LEGAL TRANSPLANTS

LEGAL TRANSPLANTS

An Approach to Comparative Law

ALAN WATSON
D.C.L.

Professor of Civil Law
The University of Edinburgh

UNIVERSITY PRESS OF VIRGINIA
CHARLOTTESVILLE

Published in the U.S.A. by
THE UNIVERSITY PRESS OF VIRGINIA

First published 1974
© 1974 Alan Watson

ISBN: 0–8139–0576–1

Library of Congress Catalog Card Number: 73–94276

Printed in Great Britain by
R. & R. Clark Ltd., Edinburgh

For
Genette and Makis Dagtoglou

PREFACE

The original impulse to write this book came from a course on Jurisprudence which I taught at the University of Virginia Law School in the Fall Semester, 1970. I should like to thank the members of that class (and of the Comparative Law classes at the University of Edinburgh) for all the stimulus they provided. Abridged versions also provoked valuable comment when presented as lectures at the Law Schools of Louisiana State University and the University of California at Berkeley, and at the Judge Advocate General's School, Charlottesville.

The whole typescript was read and criticised to my great profit by Professors Prodromos Dagtoglou, A. M. Honoré and D. Neil Mac-Cormick, Dr. Bernard Rudden and Mr. David Bentley. Other friends, among whom Professor Joseph Modrzejewski, Dr. Bernard Jackson and Mr. J. L. Barton deserve especial mention, read parts ranging from a single chapter to the greater half.

ALAN WATSON

Edinburgh
June 1973

CONTENTS

ABBREVIATIONS

A.C.	*Appeal Cases* (England)
A.D.	*Reports of the Appellate Division* (South Africa)
All ER	*All England Reports*
B.G.U.	*Aegyptische Urkunden aus den königlichen Museen zu Berlin*, i–ix (Berlin, 1895–1937)
C.	*Code of Justinian*
C.P.D.	*Reports of the Cape Provincial Division* (South Africa)
C.P.R.	C. Wessely, *Corpus Papyrorum Raineri*, i (Vienna, 1895)
C.Th.	*Codex Theodosianus*
D.	*Digest of Justinian*
E.D.L.	*Reports of the Eastern Districts Local Division* (South Africa)
G.	*Institutes of Gaius*
I.C.L.Q.	*International & Comparative Law Quarterly*
Journal of the S.P.T.L.	*Journal of the Society of Public Teachers of Law*
J.R.	*Juridical Review*
L.Q.R.	*Law Quarterly Review*
M.L.R.	*Modern Law Review*
Nov.	*Novellae of Justinian*
N.Z.L.R.	*New Zealand Law Reports*
P. Amh.	B. P. Grenfell–A. S. Hunt, *The Amherst Papyri*, i–ii (London, 1900–1901)
P. Cair. Preis.	F. Preisigke, *Griechische Urkunden des ägyptischen Museums zu Kairo* (Schriften der Wissenschaftlichen Gesellschaft Strassburg, no. 8, 1911)
P. Flor.	G. Vitelli–D. Comparetti, *Papiri Fiorentini* i–iii (Milan, 1905–1915)
P. Gen.	J. Nicole, *Les Papyrus de Genève* (Geneva, 1896–1906)
P. Grenf.	B. P. Grenfell, *An Alexandrian Erotic Fragment and other Greek Papyri* (Oxford, 1896)
P. Lips.	L. Mitteis, *Griechische Urkunden der Papyrussammlung zu Leipzig* (Leipzig, 1906)

P. Lond.	F. G. Kenyon–H. I. Bell, *Greek Papyri in the British Museum*, i–v (London, 1893–1917)
P. Oxy.	B. P. Grenfell–A. S. Hunt, *The Oxyrhynchus Papyri* i– (London, 1898–)
P. Rainer	*Mitteilungen aus der Sammlung Erzherzog Rainer*, i–vi (Vienna, 1887–1897)
P. Rein.	T. Reinach, *Papyrus grecs et démotiques* (Paris, 1905)
P.S.I.	G. Vitelli, etc., *Papiri greci e latini* i– (Florence, 1912–)
P. Strassb.	F. Preisigke, *Griechische Papyrus der Universitäts- und Landesbibliothek zu Strassburg*, i–ii (Leipzig, 1906–1920)
P. Théad.	P. Jouguet, *Papyrus de Théadelphie* (Paris, 1911)
Rhein. Mus.	*Rheinisches Museum für Philologie*
R.I.D.A.	*Revue Internationale des Droits de l'Antiquité*
S.A.	*South African Law Reports*
S.B.	F. Preisigke–F. Bihbel, *Sammelbuch griechischer Urkunden aus Ägypten*, i–v (Strassburg, etc., 1915–1950)
S.C.	*Session Cases* (Scotland)
T.P.D.	*Reports of the Transvaal Provincial Division*
T.v.R.	*Tijdschrift voor Rechtsgeschiedenis*
W.L.R.	*Weekly Law Reports* (England)
Z.S.S.	*Zeitschrift der Savigny-Stiftung* (*romanistische Abteilung*)

CHAPTER I

COMPARATIVE LAW AS AN ACADEMIC DISCIPLINE

What is Comparative Law? The question is often put:[1] the range of replies is startling. An extreme but not uncommon opinion is that it does not exist. More than one comparative lawyer – who, of course, will not admit the non-being of the subject – has observed that 'Comparative Law' is a strange phrase.[2] There is, it is freely conceded, no 'Comparative' branch of law in the sense in which lawyers call one branch of law, 'Family Law' or another 'Mercantile Law'. Gutteridge tells us that the emptiness of the phrase 'Comparative Law' 'has been realised by German-speaking lawyers who use the term *Rechtsvergleichung* which connotes a process of comparison and is free from any implication of the existence of a body of rules forming a separate branch or department of the law'. The same author also points out that the strangeness of the English term becomes manifest when attempts are made to define Comparative Law or to ascertain its relation to other forms of learning.

A variation which is frequently given on that answer is that 'Comparative Law' denotes a method of study and research, or is a technique.[3] But then it seems fair to ask, What is this method or technique? The student will find that the question tends to remain unanswered, and that the writer, having claimed that Comparative Law is a method, simply proceeds: 'The method called Comparative Law can be used for a variety of practical or scholarly purposes.'[4] Presumably such a

---

[1] Cf. K. Zweigert, 'Methodological Problems in Comparative Law', *Israel Law Review*, vii (1972), pp. 465ff at p. 465.

[2] E.g. R. W. Lee, 'Comparative Law and Comparative Lawyers', *Journal of the S.P.T.L.* (1936), pp. 1ff at p. 1; H. C. Gutteridge, *Comparative Law*, 2nd edit. (Cambridge, 1949), p. 1.

[3] E.g. Gutteridge, *Comparative Law*, p. 1; R. B. Schlesinger, *Comparative Law*, 3rd edit. (Brooklyn, 1970), p. 1; O. Kahn-Freund, C. Lévy and B. Rudden, *A Source-book on French Law* (Oxford, 1973), p. 1.

[4] So Schlesinger. R. David is slightly more explicit. He declares that Comparative Law is the comparative method applied in the field of legal sciences; and then immediately asks the purpose of this method in such a field: *Traité élémentaire de droit civil comparé* (Paris, 1950), p. 4.

writer is of the opinion that the nature of the method or technique is obvious. But if the nature of Comparative Law is obvious, it can only be the investigation of legal rules and procedures not of one system in isolation but in harness with the examination of the equivalent rules and procedures in at least one other system. Yet is this in itself a 'method' or a 'technique'? And if we answer Yes, it is a 'method' or a 'technique' – does the 'method' or 'technique' have to be specially and specifically learned?[5] The absence of discussion on this matter can only imply that the answer is No. We are then forced to put another question: If Comparative Law is no more than this, a method which does not have to be learned, is it an activity worthy of academic pursuit in its own right? Is it justifiable, for instance, to have a University course in a law faculty curriculum called 'Comparative Law'? The answer, it seems to me, must be No.

[At this point it is interesting to observe that – for whatever reason – some law faculties in the United Kingdom, for instance Cambridge and formerly also Oxford, which have a Professor of Comparative Law, have no undergraduate course with any such title; and that some faculties, for instance Oxford, which do have a course called 'Comparative Law' teach within it only one foreign system though comparisons with the domestic law may be required in examinations. The explanation of this is not simply that Comparative Law is thought more suitable for post-graduate students: Oxford, for quite a number of years after the establishment of a Chair, did not offer Comparative Law as a course even for the higher degree of B.C.L.]

Other jurists, however, have held that Comparative Law is not simply a method but is a science with its own distinct province.[6] But there is no agreement as to what the province is, and the debate as to whether Comparative Law is a method or a science has turned into a debate over language.[7] Moreover, theories that Comparative Law is a science now seem to lack support.[8]

[5] The chapter entitled 'The Process of Comparison' in Gutteridge, *Comparative Law*, pp. 72ff is mainly concerned with the problem of how to find the foreign law.

[6] See the references in Gutteridge, *Comparative Law*, p. 5, n. 2.

[7] M. Schmitthoff, 'The Science of Comparative Law', *C.L.J.* vii (1939–41), pp. 94ff at pp. 94f; cf. Gutteridge, *Comparative Law*, p. 5.

[8] Equally the question whether law itself is a science is not really a live issue among jurists though Sachs L.J. and Buckley L.J. appear to be of the opinion that law is a science in the same sense as chemistry and physics are sciences: *Council of Law Reporting* v. *Attorney General* [1971] 3 All ER 1029.

A more promising approach[9] has been to hold that more than one discipline is included within the term Comparative Law. E. Lambert, for instance, was responsible for a three-fold division;[10] Descriptive Comparative Law, Comparative History of Law and Comparative Legislation (or comparative jurisprudence proper). The first of these 'is the inventory of the systems of the past and present as a whole as well as of individual rules which these systems establish for the several categories of legal relations'. Comparative History of Law, Lambert tells us, 'is closely allied to ethnological jurisprudence, folklore, legal sociology and philosophy of law. It endeavours to bring out through the establishment of a universal history of law the rhythms or natural laws of the succession of social phenomena, which direct the evolution of legal institutions.' And he adds that 'its students have been up to the present principally interested in the reconstitution of the most obscure phases of the legal history of human societies'.[11] The third branch, Comparative Legislation, 'represents the effort to define the common trunk on which present national doctrines of law are destined to graft themselves as a result of both of the development of the study of law as a social science, and of the awakening of an international legal consciousness'. J. H. Wigmore,[12] in his turn, also divided Comparative Law into three: Comparative Nomoscopy, which is the description of systems of law; Comparative Nomothetics, which is the analysis of the merits of the systems; and Comparative Nomogenetics, which is the study of the development of the world's legal ideas and systems.

We shall be here concerned with an approach similar to that of Lambert and Wigmore but it is not proposed to look for an all-embracing definition or an enumeration of parts. The aim is more limited; namely to determine what – if anything – Comparative Law is or should be as an academic activity worthy of pursuit in its own right and with its own proper boundaries. The answer to the question, as will be seen, has more than mere pedagogic interest.

[9] To some extent it is a related approach.

[10] See now his entry in *Encyclopaedia of the Social Sciences*, iv (London, 1931), pp. 126ff.

[11] See also Lambert's discussion of *histoire comparative* in his *La Fonction du droit civil comparé*, i (Paris, 1903), pp. 913ff. The theory is untenable in so far as it involves the idea that certain principles are common to all systems of law; cf. infra, pp. 12ff.

[12] 'A New Way of Teaching Comparative Law', *Journal of the S.P.T.L.* (1926), pp. 6ff; *Panorama of the World's Legal Systems* (Washington, 1936).

But first of all, to clear the ground, we must say what Comparative Law (as an independent academic discipline) is not.

To begin with, Comparative Law is not the study of one foreign legal system or of part of one foreign system. A general course at a British or American University of French Private Law or a detailed study of French Contract Law may have great intellectual and practical value but it remains a course of French Law not Comparative Law. No doubt it is impossible to follow such a course without reflecting on, and making comparisons with, one's own law, and indeed, without increasing one's understanding of one's own law, but this does not change the essential nature of the course as French Law. This remains true even where an expressed aim of the course is the insight it gives into the domestic system.

Secondly, an elementary account of various legal systems or of various 'families' of systems cannot be decently regarded as the proper pursuit of Comparative Law as an academic activity. The description lacks the necessary intellectual content.

Thirdly and more arguably Comparative Law cannot be primarily a matter of drawing comparisons. Those who would disagree with this proposition proceed from one of two starting points. They may start from an individual legal problem which they consider to be the same in more than one jurisdiction and examine the legal response to it.[13] As one scholar has put it, 'The fact that the problem is one and the same warrants the comparability.'[14] Or they may take a branch of law, say Contract, and investigate in detail the differences and similarities of the individual rules. But it is very doubtful if the comparisons are justifiable in academic terms[15] as Comparative Law, whether the starting point is the legal problem or the branch of the law. Variations in the political, moral, social and economic values which exist between any two societies make it hard to believe that many legal problems are the same for both except on a technical level. For instance, the legal problem of rent restriction is not the same both in a country where rented accommodation is common and in a country where it is less common; the problem of alimony for divorced wives in a jurisdiction

[13] E.g. Schmitthoff, 'Science', p. 96.

[14] M. Salomon, *Grundlegung zur Rechtsphilosophie*, 2nd edit. (Berlin, 1925), p. 30; quoted with approval by Schmitthoff, loc. cit.

[15] The comparisons may well be justified in practical terms, but then the nature of the investigation will be very different: cf. infra, pp. 17f. For problems of comparability in a different field see R. Robertson and L. Taylor, *Deviance, Crime and Socio-Legal Control: Comparative Perspectives* (London, 1973), pp. 19ff.

where it is usual for women to work differs from that in a country where women do not have jobs;[16] that problem and the proper legal response to it may also be altered by the availability or otherwise of crèches and nursery schools for young children; the legal problem of the enforceability of contracts against minors will vary with the affluence of the society, the age at which young people become accustomed to living on credit, and the extent to which residing away from their parents is prevalent. Perhaps on rare occasions one might find that the problem was identical or at least very similar, as when the matter at issue concerns international business.[17] Yet when the starting point is the problem the weight of the investigation will always be primarily on the comparability of the problem, only secondarily on the comparability of the law; and any discipline founded on such a starting point will be sociology rather than law.[18]

[It might be opposed to the foregoing that the nature of a legal problem likewise varies from one individual to another within a legal jurisdiction, and that the differences in the factors affecting the problem can be greater between two Englishmen, one a wealthy London business man, the other a hill farmer in the Pennines, than between the Londoner and a Parisian counterpart. But where this is so, the sociology rather than law becomes still more pronounced. Moreover, when more jurisdictions than one are being considered together, the unit becomes the particular jurisdiction; that jurisdiction becomes the individual as it were, with all his inherent contradictions of character, aims and social rôles.]

When the starting point is a branch of law, the difficulty arising from the variations of political, moral, social and economic factors for any valid comparison recedes to some extent, but is still very much present. Moreover, except where the systems are closely related the differences in legal values may be so extreme as to render virtually meaningless the discovery that systems have the same or a different rule. Where the legal systems are closely related as in certain states in America, a comparison of legal rules may be intellectually meaningful, but the minor nature of the differences which exist may limit the significance of the investigation. It is not surprising that Gutteridge

[16] And where they have social security as of right, and where they have not.

[17] See the interesting instance adduced by O. Kahn-Freund, 'Comparative Law as an Academic Subject', *L.Q.R.* lxxxii (1966), pp. 40ff at pp. 46f.

[18] I should not be taken as implying that knowledge of the legal rules of different systems has not an important rôle to play in sociology of law.

can write in the preface to his book on *Comparative Law*, 'No special form of technique seems to be called for if the comparison is, for instance, between Australian and Canadian law or between English law and the law of the United States.'[19]

Yet, despite the preceding paragraphs, it should be readily conceded that teaching courses of considerable educational value can be constructed on the basis of comparisons of a branch of law in various legal systems. The merit of such courses lies in alerting the student to the many approaches which are conceivable, and this merit may exist independently of any theoretical structure which would give deeper meaning to the comparisons. Likewise it should be conceded that certain legal concepts – causation is one good example[20] – and their actual delineation in various systems can be the object of an enquiry on the highest intellectual and systematic plane. But the point of these enquiries is to explicate a concept of great importance in law by a careful examination of the way in which it operates in the detailed context of differing legal systems (as well as the way in which it is discussed by theorists). Then, I venture to suggest, the study is primarily jurisprudential and is support for the widely held view that much of jurisprudence is unthinkable without comparisons from various systems.

Comparative Law, then, if it is to be an intellectual discipline in its own right, is something other than the study of one foreign system (with glances at one's own), an overall look at the world's systems or comparison of individual rules or of branches of law as between two or more systems, and I would suggest that it is the study of the relationship of one legal system and its rules with another. The nature of any such relationship, the reasons for the similarities and the differences, is discoverable only by a study of the history of the systems or of the rules; hence in the first place, Comparative Law is Legal History concerned with the relationship between systems. But one cannot treat Comparative Law simply as a branch of Legal History. It must be something more. When one comes to trace the growth of these similarities and differences – how, for instance, has it come about that France, Germany and Switzerland, all deriving their law from Justinian's *Corpus Iuris Civilis*, have each different rules on the passing of risk and property in sale? – one finds oneself better able to understand

[19] p. xi.
[20] See, e.g., H. A. Hart and A. M. Honoré, *Causation in the Law* (Oxford, 1959).

the particular factors which shape legal growth and change. Indeed this may be the easiest approach to an appreciation of how law normally evolves. This seems a proper field of study for Comparative Law. So, in the second instance, I suggest that Comparative Law is about the nature of law, and especially about the nature of legal development.

These two elements coming from a study of the relationship between systems – Legal History and the step beyond into Jurisprudence – are, I submit, the essential ingredients of Comparative Law as an intellectual discipline in its own right. The importance of the history behind the legal rules has, in fact, long been recognised by comparatists, and history is prominent in the writings of the most distinguished practitioners of the art; witness, for instance, J. P. Dawson, *Unjust Enrichment* (Boston, 1951): F. H. Lawson, *A Common Lawyer looks at the Civil Law* (Ann Arbor, 1953): J. H. Merryman, *The Civil Law Tradition* (Stanford, 1969): R. David, *Les Grands Systèmes de droit contemporains*, 4th edit. (Paris, 1971). O. Kahn-Freund can say of one particular instance in German and English law, 'Four hundred years of legal and political history are reflected in the difference of techniques'.[21] F. Pringsheim declares roundly, 'comparative law without the history of law is an impossible task'.[22]

If this approach is right and Comparative Law is best regarded as a study of the relationship between systems of law, then it follows that where there is no relationship there can be no Comparative Law, and any comparison drawn between rules will be arbitrary and without systematic worth. It thus becomes important to establish the nature of possible relationships. In the forefront, above all, stands the historical relationship: where one system or one of its rules derives from another system, probably with modifications; where more than one system or rules of such systems derive from a further system; or (where derive is too strong a term) when one system exerts influence on another. In any general or introductory work this type of relationship should have pride of place, first because the relationship itself is more obvious than any other type, secondly because the degree of borrowing and adaptation is more easily spotted, thirdly because the relevant factors in the development can be isolated more simply, and fourthly because in the Western world borrowing (with adaptation) has been the usual way of legal development. On this last point S. F. C. Milsom has

---

[21] 'Comparative Law', p. 47.
[22] 'The inner Relationship between English and Roman Law' in *Gesammelte Schriften*, i (Heidelberg, 1961), 1961), pp. 76ff at p. 78.

spoken clearly: 'Societies largely invent their constitutions, their political and administrative systems, even in these days their economies; but their private law is nearly always taken from others. Twice only have the customs of European peoples been worked up into intellectual systems. The Roman system has served two separate civilisations. The common law, governing daily relationships in very various modern societies, has developed without a break from its beginnings in a society utterly different from any of them.'[23]

A second type of relationship is what F. Pringsheim has called the 'inner relationship'.[24] This rests not on any actual historical contact,[25] but on a spiritual and psychical relationship and on an undeniable similarity between the peoples – as Pringsheim thinks – or between their development. Comparative Law can proceed from this inner relationship but one must always bear in mind that the relationship itself is an unproveable hypothesis.[26] In terms of Western civilisation, this inner relationship is to be found above all between Roman and English Law, and comparisons between the two have long been popular and fruitful.[27] But the difficulties and dangers in this branch of study are obvious: the relationship cannot be closely defined, its nature will not always be apparent, it will not exist in all areas or at all periods of development, and above all there is no reasonably objective way of determining the importance of the similarities and differences which are observed. The great value of this branch of the study lies in the light which it can shed on major legal matters. When English law has not been influenced by Roman law it is of small significance that a detail is the same or is different in the two systems. But, in contrast, the absence of the trust in Roman law and its prominence and usefulness in English law should make us more aware of the nature of the trust and of the factors in its development. One might also come to understand Roman law better by analysing the lack of the trust, the factors making it unnecessary or impossible for the Romans, and the institutions which took its place. Conversely the remedies against unjust enrichment in Roman law and the general lack of such until recently in the common law should make us more alive to various aspects of

---

[23] *Historical Foundations of the Common Law* (London, 1969), p. ix.

[24] 'Inner Relationship', p. 77.

[25] Though influence there may have been.

[26] So, rightly, Pringsheim.

[27] Cf. above all, W. W. Buckland and A. D. McNair, *Roman Law and Common Law*, 2nd edit., by F. H. Lawson (Cambridge, 1952).

both systems. Likewise, much might be gained by an investigation into the rôle of statutes and the prominence of (what one might loosely call) case-law at Rome and in England: or into the relative degree of abstraction in juridical discussion and formulation.

A third relationship might be suggested by those scholars who believe that all legal systems in their young days pass through the same or similar stages of development. The general proposition is unsound as we shall see,[28] though between various early systems a historical relationship exists.[29]

Comparative Law then, as an academic discipline in its own right, is a study of the relationship, above all the historical relationship, between legal systems or between rules of more than one system; and this is the subject of the present book. This book is written in the belief that in the past the boundaries of Comparative Law have been drawn too widely, and that they should define an area akin to that of comparative linguistics; that is, they should be concerned with similarities and differences in the context of a historical relationship. Yet to prevent misunderstanding it should be stressed at this stage that a knowledge of foreign systems of law – of a sort which would not be included within such a conception of Comparative Law – can be very valuable. It can have educational value as was mentioned earlier:[30] and practical value, for instance when law reformers searching for better law for their own system look at other solutions. The investigation need have no systematic basis to produce fruitful results.[31] And it can have academic value, for instance when a scholar who has reached particular conclusions about a development in one system can confirm the possibility of such a development by the knowledge that something similar happened elsewhere.[32]

[28] Infra, pp. 12ff.

[29] For an example see infra, pp. 22ff.

[30] Supra, p. 6.

[31] See infra, pp. 17ff. Interestingly although such a look at foreign systems is not Comparative Law as here understood, the looking itself can become a proper object of study for Comparative Law.

[32] Cf. infra, pp. 17ff.

CHAPTER 2

THE PERILS OF COMPARATIVE LAW

In a book on Comparative Law it may seem perverse to write a prominent chapter on 'The Perils', but it is important to stress the dangers inherent in the study and its limitations. Much has been claimed for Comparative Law yet so far it has contributed relatively little to the understanding of law or legal development. At times sadly it has obscured the truth. An awareness of the perils, whether they are inevitable or only normal, should lead to a more just appreciation of the contribution which Comparative Law can make. Some of the dangers stem from the comparative method in general; others are particular to Comparative Law.

To begin with, Comparative Law is superficial. As astounding as this may seem as a bald statement, the fact is admitted by some leading comparatists. F. H. Lawson has indeed gone further and claimed 'Now, in a sense, a comparative lawyer is bound to be superficial; he would soon lose himself in the sands of scholarship.'[1] The explanation is patent: it is hard enough to know in detail one branch of the law of one system, but to know the history of that branch and its relationship with that of some other system (and thus to possess a knowledge of the history of that as well) is well-nigh impossible. A University course on even one foreign legal system will normally demand less knowledge than would be expected in a similar course on the native law. A general book written on French law for an English audience may properly be much more highly regarded than would a book of equivalent scope on English law for the same readers.[2] Naturally some studies will be less superficial than others.

This peril of Comparative Law is then compounded with another, even more serious, getting the foreign law wrong.[3] Error of law is probably more common in Comparative Law than in any other branch

---

[1] 'The Field of Comparative Law', *J.R.* lxi (1949), pp. 16ff at p. 16.

[2] Here I am thinking specifically of the rightly famous Amos and Walton, *Introduction to French Law*, 3rd edit., by F. H. Lawson, A. E. Anton and L. Neville Brown (Oxford, 1967).

[3] Cf. H. C. Gutteridge, *Comparative Law*, 2nd edit. (Cambridge, 1949), p. 15, and the passage he quotes from Lord Bacon.

of legal study. Again the reason is only too plain. Too much has to be taken on trust from other writers, including other comparatists, too often knowledge is derived from too few original sources, and too frequently linguistic deficiences interpose a formidable barrier between the scholar and his subject. This last aspect must be emphasised. What in other contexts would be regarded as a good knowledge of a foreign language may not be adequate for the comparatist. Homonyms present traps.[4] The French *contrat, domicile, tribunal administratif, notaire, prescription* and *juge de paix*, are not the English 'contract', 'domicile', 'administrative tribunal', 'notary public', 'prescription' and 'justice of the peace'.

The fragility of conclusions dependent on a superficial knowledge combined with frequent error of law should be underlined.

A third peril is that Comparative Law can scarcely be systematic.[5] Again we are indebted to Lawson for the insight: 'I do not see how a comparison between two laws can be systematic.'[6] Hence even where there is a relationship between two systems – as explained in the preceding chapter – there will always be a considerable element of selection in the objects of study. In the very nature of things the choice can scarcely ever be made in full knowledge of all the relevant facts. Some degree of arbitrariness will inevitably ensue and be reflected in any general conclusions. To some variable and indefinable extent any study of Comparative Law will be subjective, and no objective test will demonstrate that the aspects considered were the most appropriate and the only ones appropriate. But luckily the converse does not hold. Grossly inappropriate or unhelpful investigations or comparisons are apparent or easily demonstrable.

Another weakness is that the systems chosen for study may have no proper relationship, and the conclusions will be lacking in significance. Even worse, the faults of this approach may be compounded and the systems be examined at different points in their evolution. Though this last danger has long been recognised by comparatists[7] it remains distressingly tempting.

[4] This is rightly stressed by O. Kahn-Freund, 'Comparative Law as an Academic Subject', *L.Q.R.* lxxxii (1966), pp. 40ff at pp. 52f. The examples are taken from him.

[5] At least there is no single system, no set of criteria which would be useful for all purposes, or acceptable to all scholars.

[6] In the preface to his (the second) edition of W. W. Buckland and A. D. McNair, *Roman Law and Common Law* (Cambridge, 1952), p. xii.

[7] Cf., e.g., M. Schmitthoff, 'The Science of Comparative Law', *C.L.J.* vii (1939–41), pp. 94ff at pp. 96f and the references he gives.

This leads on to one of the greatest (and strangest) perils of Comparative Law, the desire to see a particular legal pattern common at least in outline to all, or to many divergent, systems. This affects most strongly scholars concerned with the early history of societies. F. Pringsheim expresses the attitude exactly: 'A natural relationship exists at an early stage between all primitive legal systems; each system during its youth seems to pass through a similar process before the peculiarities of the nation are imposed upon its juridical order.'[8] This theory, in one form or another, has existed since at least the writings of Sir Henry Maine, but can appear plausible only if fundamental facts are misunderstood or misrepresented. The most famous and influential work of Maine is undoubtedly his *Ancient Law* (first published in 1861) and in the Preface he relates that he has of necessity taken Roman Law as a typical system of ancient law and that he may appear to have drawn from that system a disproportionate number of examples. Now it has been observed that whereas *Ancient Law* is often discussed in Jurisprudence and Anthropology courses it is little used in classes of Roman law. The reason is that Maine's statements on Roman law are not reliable. Nor can accuracy on legal facts be considered an attribute of those who have followed Maine's approach.The objection is not that these over-all presentations will not satisfy the expert in a particular early system,[9] but that the appearance of similar development is achieved only by the grossest misstatement of relevant legal facts. At times it is as if a comparative anatomist were to say that lions and ants are similar and are at a comparable level of development since both are warmblooded, have six legs and are always winged.

This matter must be considered more fully since if a 'natural relationship' did exist between all legal systems at some stage in their development then a proper part of Comparative Law in its own right would be the study of that relationship. That a historical relationship exists between some early systems is undeniable and is a proper study for the comparatist. And one should admit that often early systems which have no historical relationship display similarities in some of their aspects – it would be astonishing if at times different peoples did not

[8] 'The Inner Relationship between English and Roman Law', now in *Gesammelte Schriften*, i (Heidelberg, 1961), pp. 76ff at p. 76.

[9] This point is made in response to B. S. Jackson's review of A. S. Diamond, *Primitive Law Past and Present* (London, 1971) in *L.Q.R.* (1972), pp. 266ff, when he says (at p. 270): 'Like the works of Maine, even this much improved presentation will not satisfy the expert. But that should not blind us to its very considerable merits.'

have the same basic response to a situation. What is here denied is that one can set up a theory of general legal development applicable to all or many unrelated societies.[10]

We must attack the theory on its own ground, take the most learned, full and modern version of the theory and show that in the case of at least one system – we need not consider more – the view propounded of its nature at one stage of development is quite wrong, and that it is apparently the theory of evolution which has formed the author's views of that legal system, not the evidence which directly concerns the system.

[It may be thought – rightly – that this approach is methodologically not perfect, but there is probably no alternative. When a theory is not based on firm principles it may not be possible to disprove it by objective abstract argument. Here, moreover, what is at issue is sound observed fact. The problem is that there are so many variations in material culture and economic rating that simply to point to two or more instances where legal development is different will only be met by the rejoinder that the peoples at the times studied were not at the same point of development.[11] Another, perhaps even greater, difficulty is that quite a few scholars (including Pringsheim) who have expressed their belief in the theory have not shown how far they accept it in any developed form, or indeed precisely what they mean in historical terms. But the theory can only be established – and can only be rebutted – if it is developed. It is for these reasons that we must take issue on ground chosen by the main proponent of the theory, and show that in one important instance (for him) the legal position described by him derives from his theory and not from evidence.[12]]

Accordingly we must consider for a moment A. S. Diamond's *Primitive Law Past and Present* (London 1971)[13] and we will single out for discussion his chapter on the Roman Twelve Tables.[14]

According to Roman tradition their earliest codification, the XII Tables, was produced in 451 and 450 B.C. Though strong doubts were

[10] That idea has great fascination and will not easily die.

[11] The variations in material culture and economic rating should also prove an extreme obstacle to those scholars who wish to establish the theory on a complex evolutionary basis; cf., e.g., Jackson, 'Review of Diamond'.

[12] The weakness inherent in this attack on the theory is not altered in character if the base of the attack is widened to include demonstration of the factual inaccuracies of other proponents of the theory.

[13] Cf., e.g., Jackson, 'Review of Diamond', p. 270.

[14] pp. 114ff.

expressed on the accuracy of this tradition around the turn of the present century by Pais and Lambert, both of whom favoured a later date, the tradition is broadly accepted by every single living Roman lawyer. Diamond, who points to the lack of satisfactory reliable evidence for early Roman history, does not believe that the XII Tables were a legal code: 'What we have is a school-book of the pontifical schools chiefly containing legal maxims handed down and developed by successive copyists, and dating from an age when there were few other documents by which to test and correct it. Its contents would tend to become fixed about 280 B.C. in the days of Appius Claudius the Censor, when history began, and especially by 250 B.C. when the general population began to use writing . . .'[15]

But what positive reasons does Diamond give for this theory on the XII Tables, which is so at variance with the scholarship in the field? First he claims that 'by the standard of the Late Codes[16] it is difficult to suppose that it consisted, as a whole, of legislation . . .', and he says in justification that it has few or no express sanctions. Secondly, it is this absence of express sanctions which indicates to him that the XII Tables are the contents of a school-book 'comparable with such a school law-book as the surviving Neo-Assyrian copies of the old Babylonian "ana ittišu" '.[17] But it should be observed that for the positive side of his theory Diamond gives no reason based on the internal history of Rome or of Roman law. His arguments are based on the nature of Late Codes and a Babylonian school-book. Not only, therefore, are the arguments drawn from the experience of other peoples, but from distant peoples at that, ranging from the non-Indo-European inhabitants of ancient Babylonia around the early second millennium B.C. to Englishmen of between A.D. 1100 and 1250.[18] Accordingly the arguments can have no weight except to those who already believe in the pattern of development. Moreover, as even a cursory glance at the surviving XII Tables will show, it is just not the case that the codification has 'few or no express sanctions'. Even later, as it happens, not all Roman forms of legislation express a sanction.[19]

[15] pp. 122f.
[16] For Diamond, 'The "Late Codes" is the name given in this book to all codes of law of the state of material culture represented by the scanty English codes between A.D. 1100 and 1250', p. 82.
[17] p. 120.　　　　　[18] Diamond, *Primitive Law*, pp. 82ff.
[19] For the form *Ne quis fecisse velit*, see D. Daube, *Forms of Roman Legislation* (Oxford, 1956), pp. 37ff. The early edict of the curule aediles on the sale of beasts which is recorded in Aulus Gellius, *N.A.* 4. 2. 1, also has no express sanction.

Perhaps even more surprising than Diamond's decision to accept a view contrary to that of all contemporary Roman law scholars on the XII Tables is his complete failure to discuss or even, so far as we can tell, consider the arguments which have persuaded those scholars that the XII Tables were a code of about 451 B.C. Naturally the accuracy of the Roman tradition was very much discussed following the doubts of Pais and Lambert and it has been observed, for instance, that some provisions point to a time about 450 B.C. A judgement debtor could be sold *trans Tiberim*, which must mean abroad into non-Latin (Etruscan) territory, in which alone would the citizen lose his citizenship and freedom. Hence at the time in question the Tiber was the frontier with the Etruscans; and this can only be after the Etruscans lost control over Latium but before the Romans had crossed the Tiber and attacked Veii. The numerous restrictions on luxurious mourning are best explained as a reaction against the famous contemporary Etruscan luxury in such matters, which would live on at Rome for some little time after the expulsion of the Tarquins. Over-luxurious mourning, moreover, could not have remained a living problem requiring legislation for long after 450 B.C. with the enormous decline in Roman economic standards which is attested by archaeology.[20]

It thus appears that in this instance the doctrine of a general pattern of development has come, in the work of its proponent, to obscure the actual development of the legal system. More generally, the weakness of the theory of a general pattern of development has been shown, at least as it is exemplified by its most erudite supporter.

A final peril of Comparative Law is that, even when legal facts are proved or appear to be proved for one system, one may argue too easily from them to a similar situation in another system which has a relationship with it. The method, of course, is itself unobjectionable and can be used with great profit; the perils are that the results obtained by it cannot be absolutely certain,[21] that it is extremely difficult to judge the right extent to which one can draw satisfactory parallels and it is easy to overstep the mark, and that it is often tempting to base further argument and deduction on the results.

[20] For these and other arguments see now above all, F. Wieacker, 'Die XII Tafeln in ihrem Jahrhundert', *Entretiens sur l'antiquité classique*, xiii, *Les origines de la République Romaine* (Fondation Hardt, Vandœuvres-Genève, 1967), pp. 293ff, especially at pp. 310ff.

[21] Cf., e.g., P. Birks, 'English Beginnings and Roman Parallels', *Irish Jurist*, vi (1971), pp. 147ff at p. 162.

CHAPTER 3

THE VIRTUES OF COMPARATIVE LAW

So far in this book we have been concerned with Comparative Law as a discipline in its own right, and have given it what others may consider a rather narrow sphere; and with the perils of Comparative Law which we have claimed to be many and severe. To redress the balance it is proper to make more explicit the virtues first of Comparative Law, then of a knowledge of foreign law.

The prime virtue of Comparative Law is the understanding it can give of the nature of law and especially of legal development. By means of it we should be able to isolate the factors which actually have led to a real innovation in a particular society. We should also learn whether a legal rule which is transported to another system is likely to exist unchanged in its new setting. We shall discern more clearly the conditions which favour legal development both in general and in a particular direction, and the conditions which hamper development. Even when our understanding of the formal sources of law is not increased we shall have achieved a fuller insight into the facts which shape the creation of legal rules. In all this lies the justification for an academic discipline of Comparative Law. But the subject also has practical utility. It can enable those actively concerned with law reform to understand their historical rôle and their task better. They should see more clearly whether and how far it is reasonable to borrow from other systems and from which systems, and whether it is possible to accept foreign solutions with modifications or without modifications.[1]

We have – rightly, I insist – rigidly separated Comparative Law from a study of foreign law and have restricted the former as an academic discipline to a study of the relationship between different legal systems and between rules of different systems. But it is fair to acknowledge the considerable value both practical and academic to be derived from a knowledge of foreign law.[2]

[1] Cf. infra, pp. 95ff.
[2] We need not, however, list or discuss all the uses and virtues claimed for a knowledge of foreign laws: but see, e.g., H. C. Gutteridge, *Comparative Law,*

The systematic study of a foreign system of law has its own intellectual value and justification. There can also be no doubt that a knowledge of, say, French law or Roman law will enable the Englishman or Scot to understand his own system better and to discern the methods and approaches which are typical of it.[3] It is also probably right to maintain that a good systematic knowledge of one or more foreign systems is essential for anyone who wishes to engage seriously in Comparative Law: to put the case at its lowest such knowledge will greatly improve a comparatist. The systematic knowledge of a foreign system can also be of the utmost practical value to a lawyer whose work has a supra-national character or to a law reformer seeking improvements for his own national system.

But I should here like to stress the value which a knowledge of foreign law can have even when the knowledge is by no means detailed or systematic.

Even unsystematic knowledge can be very useful in a practical way for, say, law reform. A person whose function it is to consider possible improvements in the law of bankruptcy in Scotland may well set out to discover the legal approach in England, France, Sweden, South Africa, New Zealand and so on. He may have no knowledge of these systems to begin with, and at the end he may know little about them except for an outline of their bankruptcy laws. He may, indeed, have little idea of how well or how badly these laws operate. But his concern is with the improvement of bankruptcy law in Scotland. What he is looking for in his investigation of foreign systems is an idea which can be transformed into part of the law of Scotland and will there work well. A rule of Swedish law which is successful at home might be a disaster in the different circumstances existing in Scotland; a rule of French law which there works badly might provide an ideal rule for Scotland.[4]

When the available evidence for the system which a scholar, especially a legal historian, is studying points towards a particular development then his conclusions may receive some support if he can refer to

---

2nd edit. (Cambridge, 1949), pp. 23ff; R. B. Schlesinger, *Comparative Law*, 2nd edit. (London, 1960), p. xvi; R. David, *Les Grands Systèmes de droit contemporains*, 4th edit. (Paris, 1971), pp. 5ff.

[3] Cf. O. Kahn-Freund, C. Lévy and B. Rudden, *A Source-book on French Law* (Oxford, 1973), p. 1.

[4] Nothing said here is meant to deny that a law reformer with systematic knowledge of foreign law or of Comparative Law will operate more efficiently.

a similar development elsewhere. Here, too, the scholar need not have systematic knowledge of that other system nor need there even be a relationship between the two systems. The essential point to notice, however, is that the foreign system is thus used only to confirm the results already obtained in the primary system. A gap in the knowledge of the primary system cannot be filled in this way from unsystematic knowledge of a related system or even from systematic knowledge of an unrelated system.[5] This is best explained by examples. When we have no evidence on the administration of justice in very early Roman law we cannot learn much about what it was like by looking at the administration of justice among a modern African people who are supposedly at a similar stage of development. We cannot even draw conclusions as to what was *probably* the Roman approach. At the very most it may be alleged that the Roman position *might* have been similar.[6] But if the Roman evidence itself were to indicate that at a very early period there was no state enforcement of judgements and this is also true of an African people, then the information about the latter enables us to say with certainty that it is perfectly possible for a legal system to operate without state enforcement of judgements and this may make the conclusions about Roman law (from Roman evidence) appear more plausible. Again if ancient tradition provides much information on the contents of supposed laws from the regal period of Rome (which is said to have ended in 509 B.C.) and the substance of these laws and their very existence is doubted by modern scholars, but the reported substance is very similar in character to rules of English early mediaeval law, then the English evidence indicates that there is a pattern to the Roman supposed rules. What one then makes of the pattern depends on other factors and does not concern us here.

Otto Kahn-Freund tells us that 'On the professor of comparative law the gods have bestowed the most dangerous of all their gifts, the gift of freedom'.[7] And he explains that it is for the professor to decide which legal subjects and which legal systems he will compare. He cannot cover all subjects and all systems and there is no obligation to work with any particular subject or system. This holds true equally when

---

[5] For a proper criticism of over-enthusiastic gap filling see B. S. Jackson, *L.Q.R.* lxxxviii (1972), p. 269.

[6] And no further arguments can be based on the possibility of the similarity.

[7] 'Comparative Law as an Academic Subject', *L.Q.R.* lxxxii (1966), pp. 40ff at p. 41. Cf. F. H. Lawson, 'The Field of Comparative Law', *J.R.* lxi (1949), pp. 16ff at p. 16.

Comparative Law is regarded as the study of the relationship between systems or their rules. When an attempt is made, as in the next chapters, to show in concrete terms some of the investigations which might be included within Comparative Law, choices must be made.

The first choice results for us in the selection of situations involving a historical relationship and the neglect of those which concern only the 'inner relationship'. This choice is determined above all by the factors which push the historical relationship to the forefront of Comparative Law,[8] but also by the existence of an excellent book on the main instance of the inner relationship, Roman law and English law.[9]

Sweet reason decrees the second choice. We should (and shall) deal with the central issue where there is a historical relationship, namely the borrowing and transmissibility of rules from one society or system to another.

But to illustrate legal transplanting and its consequences the choices between various systems and rules are enormous. Those which are made here are arbitrary, in so far as they depend on the author's knowledge and background, and within those limits they are chosen not for themselves but for their illustrative value. The point of the examples discussed is that they are ones which have appeared particulary striking to the author. They raise the question whether one can generalise from the particular. It is hoped that the discussion of a number of striking or extreme instances will best demonstrate what has happened and can happen in legal transplanting and will bring out the consequences of legal borrowing. It should be added that no attempt has been made to find 'typical' examples since it is doubtful whether one can here talk of 'typical' instances. There are so many varieties and each example has its own characteristics.

It would be a mistake to attempt to exhaust the possibilities of any aspect of the subject: and each individual topic, it may be observed, is dealt with only in so far as it illuminates the main theme. Hence the treatment of some parts is less detailed than the treatment of others.[10] I make no apology for this unevenness of treatment.

It has been convincingly shown, above all by Karl Renner,[11] that

[8] Cf. supra, pp. 7f.

[9] Buckland and McNair, *Roman Law and Common Law*, 2nd edit., by F. H. Lawson (Cambridge, 1952).

[10] Since accuracy of legal facts seems to me crucial in Comparative Law, I will try always to refer to the most important original sources.

[11] *The Institutions of Private Law*, edited with an Introduction by O. Kahn-Freund (London, 1949).

rules of private law can have a different effect at different times within the same society. It cannot be doubted either that a rule transplanted from one country to another, from Germany to Japan, may equally operate to different effect in the two societies, even though it is expressed in apparently similar terms in the two countries. But our first concern will be with the existence of the rule, not with how it operates within the society as a result of academic or judicial interpretation. When a legal rule is transplanted from Germany to Japan it will interest us whether it can be moved unaltered, or whether, and to what extent, it undergoes changes in its formulation. Whether, how, when and how far the effect is altered though the formulation is the same, are different and more difficult matters and will not be considered here.

CHAPTER 4

INTRODUCTION TO LEGAL TRANSPLANTS

Law shows us many paradoxes. Perhaps the strangest of all is that, on the one hand, a people's law can be regarded as being special to it, indeed a sign of that people's identity, and it is in fact remarkable how different in important detail even two closely related systems might be; on the other hand, legal transplants – the moving of a rule or a system of law from one country to another, or from one people to another – have been common since the earliest recorded history.

Thus on the one hand, in 19th-century Germany Savigny could declare:[1] 'Where we first find documented history, the civil law has already a determinate character, peculiar to the people, just as have their language, manners, constitution. Indeed, these phenomena have no separate existence, they are only the particular powers and functions of an individual people, inseparably joined in nature, and appearing as particular characteristics only to our observation.' And elsewhere:[2] 'If we ask further for the subject in which and for which positive law has its existence, we find this is the people. Positive law lives in the common consciousness of the people, and therefore we have also to call it the law of the people (Volksrecht). But this should not be so understood as if it were the individual members of the people through whose arbitrary will the law is brought forth. . . . Rather it is the spirit of the people (Volksgeist), living and working in all the individuals together, which creates the positive law, which is therefore, not by accident but necessarily, one and the same law to the consciousness of each individual.' In 20th-century Scotland, T. B. Smith can open the preface to his *Short Commentary on the Law of Scotland*:[3] 'Since her Union with England in 1707 Scotland has in a sense survived as a nation by and through her Laws and Legal System.' And the most celebrated Scottish judge of the century, Lord Cooper of Culross,

---

[1] *Vom Beruf unsrer Zeit für Gesetzgebung und Rechtswissenschaft* (Heidelberg, 1814), p. 8.

[2] *System des heutigen römischen Rechts*, i (Berlin, 1840), p. 14.

[3] (Edinburgh, 1962.) Recently he has taken a less extreme attitude: 'Scottish Nationalism, Law and Self-Government', *The Scottish Debate* (London, 1970), edited by N. MacCormick, pp. 34ff.

could stoutly maintain:[4] 'The truth is that law is the reflection of the spirit of a people, and so long as the Scots are conscious that they are a people, they must preserve their law.'

Yet, on the other hand, it is an accepted fact that most of the private law of all the modern legal systems of the Western world (and also of some non-Western countries), apart from the Scandinavian, derives more or less directly from either Roman Civil Law or English Common Law. Cohen and Cohen, discussing contract, well say:[5] 'And if the diversity of theories of contract is startling, one may find equal cause for wonder and reflection in the fact that thinkers and societies that are poles apart geographically, economically, and culturally, so often agree on specific rules of contract law. The excerpts from the Civil Code of Spain showing basic contract rules equally valid in France, Chile, Columbia, Germany, Holland, Italy, Mexico, Portugal, and many other lands, and equally honored across eighteen or more centuries, offer a substantial challenge to the view that law reflects all the changes of changing economies and all the diversities of diverse civilizations. The spectacle of Pollock describing English common law by quoting whole paragraphs from a German scholar's description of the law of ancient Rome raises a real problem for those who think, with Holmes, that the common law is "not a brooding omnipresence in the sky but the articulate voice of some sovereign or quasi-sovereign that can be identified." ' And Roscoe Pound could write: 'History of a system of law is largely a history of borrowings of legal materials from other legal systems and of assimilation of materials from outside of the law.'[6]

The phenomenon of transplantation is not restricted to the modern world. There is little point in looking for the earliest known case – mere chance would determine that – but a fine early instance can be found in ancient Near Eastern provisions concerning a goring ox. One of the Laws of Eshnunna[7] (which date from at least the 18th century B.C.) provides:[8]

> If an ox (was) a gorer and the ward (authorities) have had it made known to its owner, but *he did not guard* his ox and it gored a man and caused him to die, the owner of the ox shall weigh out $\frac{2}{3}$ of a mina of silver.

[4] 'The Scottish Legal Tradition' in *Selected Papers* (Edinburgh, 1957), p. 199.

[5] *Readings in Jurisprudence and Legal Philosophy* (Boston, Toronto, 1951), p. 101.

[6] It has been asserted by some anthropologists that 'cultures develop mainly through borrowings due to chance contact', R. H. Lowie, *Primitive Society* (New York, 1920), p. 441.

[7] A city to the east of the Tigris, situated on one of its tributaries.

[8] 54/55.

> If it gored a slave and caused him to die, he shall weigh out 14 shekels of silver.

And the Babylonian Code of Hammurabi (which is not later than the early 17th century B.C.) has:[9]

> If a man's ox (was) a gorer and the ward (authorities) have had made known to him that (it was) a gorer, but he did not screen its horns, (or) did not tie up his ox and that ox gored a son of a man and caused him to die, he shall give ½ a mina of silver.

> If (the victim was) a slave of a man, he shall give ⅓ of a mina of silver.

Exodus (of uncertain date, but centuries after the Code of Hammurabi) provides:[10]

> If an ox gore a man or a woman, and he died, the ox shall surely be stoned and his flesh shall not be eaten; but the owner of the ox shall be quit. But if the ox was a gorer from beforetimes, and it has been testified to his owner and he did not keep him in and he killed a man or a woman, the ox shall be stoned and his owner also shall be put to death. If there be laid upon him a sum of money, then he shall give for the ransom of his life whatsoever is laid upon him. Whether he gored a son or gored a daughter, according to this rule shall it be done to him. If the ox gore a slave or a slave-woman: he shall give to his master thirty shekels of silver and the ox shall be stoned.

These three provisions have obvious similarities both of substance and of formulation. As to substance it is noteworthy that they relate to a situation where the ox's owner was officially[11] notified that it was a dangerous animal. The necessity of such notification to bring the consequences of a law into operation is common neither in the ancient nor the modern world.

One might further compare Eshnunna's:[12]

> If an ox gored an ox and caused it to die, both ox owners shall divide the price of the live ox and the carcass of the dead ox.

with Exodus:[13]

> And if a man's ox gored his fellow's ox and it died, then they shall sell the live ox and divide the silver of it; and the dead [ox] also they shall divide.

The basic substance of these provisions is found in no other legal

---

[9] 251/252.   [10] 21. 28-32.
[11] Hence it differs from the scienter rule of English common law.
[12] 53.   [13] 21. 35.

system. The rule has obvious advantages: no question of 'fault' in the animal arises; problems of causation – in the sense of which animal started the fight – are avoided.[14] But equally it has great disadvantages, since it seems far too narrow. No doubt it can be extended by analogy to the case where, for instance, two rams fight. But because of the assessment of damages it has no obvious application where the antagonists are of different species. And what if the dead ox was old and worthless, whereas the other was in its prime? It should be noted that in the Laws of Eshnunna and Exodus, this rule is not supplemented by others which would cover these situations. A very different approach is to be found, for instance, in Roman law.[15] The *actio de pauperie* lay against an owner whose animal had caused damage, for the amount of the loss or for the surrender of the animal. When rams or bulls fought and one killed the other, Quintus Mucius, consul of 95 B.C., drew a distinction: if the one which attacked died there was no action, if the one which did not attack died the action would lie.[16, 17]

Now these five provisions which we have looked at from Eshnunna, the Code of Hammurabi and Exodus show such similarities of formulation and of substance that some connection, though distant, must exist between them. The nature of the similarities of style and substance is such that they exclude the possibility of parallel legal development. Probably they share an ultimate common source.[18] Thus, legal transplants are already to be found in remote antiquity and were probably not uncommon. An adherent of the 'Volksgeist', however, will find comfort in the more or less marked differences which also exist between the provisions.[19]

[14] There is, though, a difference in the two texts here. The Hebrew in Exodus does simply say 'it died' whereas in Eshnunna the verb *uš-ta-mi-it* is in the causative form, 'caused it to die'.

[15] Roman law is cited to show a different (and better) approach, and it is not being suggested that a comparable relationship exists between the Near Eastern provisions and the Roman rules.   [16] D. 9. 1. 1. 11 (Ulpian 18 *ad ed.*)

[17] For vengeance wreaked on animals which caused harm see the long passage from J. G. Frazer quoted by T. H. Gaster, *Myth, Legend, and Custom in the Old Testament* (New York, 1969), pp. 243ff and the notes on pp. 387f.

[18] For all this see, above all, R. Yaron, 'The Goring Ox in Near Eastern Laws', *Israel Law Review*, i (1966), pp. 396ff; cf. R. Haase, 'Die Behandlung von Tierschäden in den Keilschriftrechten', *R.I.D.A.* xiv (1967), pp. 11ff.

[19] A similar approach is to be found in M. Greenberg, 'Some Postulates of Biblical Criminal Law', *Yehezkel Kaufmann Jubilee Volume*, edited by M. Haran (Jerusalem, 1960), pp. 5ff.

Before looking more closely at the nature and significance of legal transplants a word of warning must be given. The old adage, 'Seek, and ye shall find' applies here with considerable force. The earliest Roman legal codification, the Twelve Tables, was made, as has been said, apparently in 451/450 B.C. According to the main Roman tradition, a delegation had first been sent abroad to study the laws of some Greek city states, including Athens to examine the Laws of Solon, but traditions of what went on in early Rome are not always reliable.[20] Most modern scholars believe that Greek influence on the code was very considerable, even if they deny that a delegation went to Greece (or existed at all) and consider the main point of contact to be Magna Graecia.[21] A few jurists apparently have reservations.[22] The argumentation is inevitably indirect in view of the nature of the sources: similarities between a few individual legal provisions are not particulary significant, nor necessarily are statements from a much later writer that a certain provision was the result of direct borrowing.[23]

[20] The main relevant sources are Livy, 3. 31. 8; 3. 32. 6; Dionysius of Halicarnassus, 10. 51. 5; 10. 52. 4; Cicero, de leg. 2. 23. 59; 2. 25. 64. See also the texts referred to by F. Wieacker, 'Die XII Tafeln in ihrem Jahrhundert'. *Entretiens sur l'antiquité classique, xiii, Les origines de la République Romaine* (Fondation Hardt, Vandœuvres-Genève, 1967), pp. 293ff at pp. 338ff.

[21] E.g. Wieacker, 'XII Tafeln', pp. 330ff, and the authors he cites, p. 330, n.2; 'Solon und die XII Tafeln', *Studi in onore di E. Volterra*, iii (Milan, 1971), pp. 757ff; E. Norden, *Aus altrömischen Priesterbüchern* (Lund, 1939), pp. 254ff, and 262ff; L. R. Palmer, *The Latin Language* (London, 1954), p. 64; J. Delz, 'Der griechische Einfluß auf die Zwölftafelgesetzgebung', *Museum Helveticum*, xxiii (1966), pp. 69ff.

[22] E.g. V. Arangio-Ruiz, *Storia del diritto romano*, 7th edit. (Naples, 1957), p. 56.

[23] But special reference must be made to Cicero's claim in *de re pub.* II. 23. 59 and II. 25. 64 that the XII Tables' provisions on mourning derive from Solon's legislation, especially the restriction to three *ricinia*: cf. Wieacker, 'XII Tafeln', pp. 345ff. It is by no means certain that Cicero is right. Thus (a) the XII Tables' *ricinia*, whatever they were – the ancients were not agreed; Festus, s.v. *Recinium*, Nonius, s.v. *Ricin⟨i⟩um* – do not seem to have been the same as Solon's ἱμάτια in Plutarch, *Solon*, 21. 5; (b) Solon's legislation talks of three ἱμάτια, the XII Tables of three *ricinia* plus a *tunicula purpurea*, so the correspondence leaves something to be desired; (c) Solon's ἱμάτια were buried with the body but can we be sure this was the case with *ricinia*? Cicero, referring to the XII Tables' provision, says, *Extenuato igitur sumptu tribus riciniis et tunicula purpurea et decem tibicinibus*. The ten flute players were certainly not buried and there may have been nothing in the code to justify Cicero's apparent assumption that the *ricinia* were. Varro (at Nonius s.v. *Ricin⟨i⟩um*) takes *ricinia* as particular mourning garments worn by women (not as garments laid in the grave with the corpse).

Those scholars who think there was considerable direct Greek influence on the provisions of the XII Tables now seem to rely strongly on three arguments. The first is resemblances in the substance and formulation to early Greek law codes, e.g. to that of Gortyn in Crete.[24, 25] Resemblances there certainly are, but no more than one might expect in civilisations not too disparate in their level of development.[26] As a matter of fact, in style and substance, the XII Tables are in general closer to the Laws of Lipit-Ishtar (of the first half of the 19th century B.C.) and of Eshnunna, and to the Code of Hammurabi,[27, 28] but it has never been suggested that a Roman delegation was sent to Asia Minor and Mesopotamia. The second argument is that the word *poena*, punishment or penalty, which occurs in the XII Tables[29] and is a focal word in legal vocabulary is a borrowing from the Greek – in fact Doric – ποινή. Norden,[30] indeed, rightly makes the point that the borrowing must have occurred before the XII Tables since the *decemviri* would scarcely have introduced the word into the language in this legal code. But the borrowing of the word *poena* cannot be taken as evidence of the influence of Doric law – that is, in this instance, of Magna Graecia – on Roman law. In the first place it is not absolutely certain that *poena* is a direct borrowing from Greek: it is possible, though unlikely, that it was borrowed at second hand, first passing through some intermediate language like Osco-Umbrian.[31] More important, it is extremely likely that *poena*, like the majority of early borrowings from Greek, came from the 'Volkssprache', and was borrowed to signify the punishment of a slave by his master.[32] If this view is correct, then the existence of the word *poena* in Latin before the

[24] Cf. Norden, *Priesterbüchern*, pp. 254, 257; Palmer, loc. cit.; Wieacker, 'XII Tafeln', pp. 331f, 351f.

[25] The most convenient edition, with translation, of the Laws of Gortyn is R. F. Willetts, *The Law Code of Gortyn* (Berlin, 1967).

[26] Though Gortyn then was certainly more advanced.

[27] The most convenient collection of these laws in translation is to be found in *Ancient Near Eastern Texts Relating to the Old Testament*, edited by J. B. Pritchard, 3rd edit. (Princeton, 1969), pp. 159ff.

[28] It would be pointless to produce individual provisions for either side. The codes must be looked at as a whole.

[29] 8. 4.

[30] *Priesterbüchern*, p. 254; Palmer, loc. cit.; Wieacker, 'XII Tafeln', p. 352.

[31] Cf., e.g., G. Ciulei, *Rhein. Mus.* xli (1942), pp. 287f; G. Devoto, *Storia della lingua di Roma*, 2nd reprint (Bologna, 1944), p. 21.

[32] Cf. A. Ernout and A. Meillet, *Dictionnaire étymologique de la langue latine*, ii, 4th edit. (Paris, 1960), p. 518.

time of the XII Tables need not point to any knowledge at Rome of Greek law codes. The third argument is from the intensity of Greek influence on Rome before the middle of the 5th century B.C., which is extremely clear in religion, arts and crafts and trade.[33] This influence in many fields is indeed intense, but it would be dangerous to infer that there was also influence on Roman law.[34] One of the most marked (and strangest) characteristics of that law, at least in times for which we have more evidence, is its independence from foreign influence. Thus the last two hundred years of the Republic are the time when Greek influence on Rome was strongest, but it would be hard to find a single legal rule which owed its existence to Greek contacts.[35, 36] I should like to emphasise at this point that I am denying neither that a delegation was sent to study Greek laws nor that there were considerable Greek importations in the XII Tables.[37] Nor am I asserting such. The point is simply that the main arguments which are used to confirm the Roman tradition are not strong, and that there is no evidence.[38]

One final preliminary point. A successful legal transplant – like that of a human organ – will grow in its new body, and become part of that body just as the rule or institution would have continued to develop in its parent system. Subsequent development in the host system should not be confused with rejection. To take one example: When the Roman *lex Aquilia* of 287 B.C. which gave an action when there was financial loss resulting from wrongful injury to property, including slaves, was received in the later states of Western Europe it was,

[33] Cf. for all, Wieacker, 'XII Tafeln', pp. 334f.

[34] Indeed, it should be observed that Wieacker himself thinks the reception of Greek law less surprising than that the XII Tables remained so completely Roman: 'XII Tafeln', p. 353.

[35] Though it is often suggested that Greek influence was important in the development of the delict *iniuria*.

[36] The matter is further discussed, infra, pp. 75ff.

[37] It is possible that there was some Semitic influence on early Roman law and that this has been consistently ignored or underestimated; cf. J. J. Rabinowitz, *Jewish Law, its Influence on the Development of Legal Institutions* (New York, 1956), pp. 1ff; and R. Yaron, 'Semitic Elements in Early Rome', in *Daube Noster*, edited by A. Watson (Edinburgh and London, 1974), pp. 343ff.

[38] Another instance of 'Seek and ye shall find' occurred in the earlier years of this century after the discovery of the Code of Hammurabi when many scholars thought they could trace considerable influence of it on the Old Testament; cf. for literature and a criticism of that approach, B. S. Jackson, 'Evolution and Foreign Influence in Ancient Law', *American Journal of Comparative Law*, xvi (1968), pp. 372ff. at p. 373.

perhaps not unreasonably, treated as covering injuries to free men. Roman analogous actions, *actiones utiles* and *actiones in factum*, had already been given so as to extend effectively the scope of the *lex Aquilia* in this way.[39] The action on the *lex Aquilia* at Rome lay only in respect of financial loss and hence, though there is no direct evidence, it would not lie for mere disfigurement. This is expressly stated in Justinian's Digest for another action:[40] 'but no valuation is made of scars or deformity since the body of free men admits of no valuation'.[41] The Dutch jurists of the 17th century, who accepted that the *lex Aquilia* had been received in their land, did give an action for disfigurement[42] although they admitted that this was contrary to Roman law.[43] This was the result of a fairly slow development which began at least as early as Albericus de Rosate in the 14th century, but we need here go no further back than the Spaniard Antonio Gomez in the 16th century who seems to be the earliest jurist who is commonly cited by the Roman-Dutch writers on this point. He declares[44] that a free man has no action on account of a scar but adds that a scar and deformity would in the case of a woman be properly estimated, at least when she was not married, because on this account she would find a husband whom she could marry with greater difficulty, and with a larger dowry.[45] Presumably for Gomez the measure of damages would be the amount by which the dowry would have to be increased in order to find a suitable husband. His qualification, *saltem*, 'at least when she

---

[39] Cf. D. 9. 2. 13pr (Ulpian *18 ad ed.*). *Liber homo suo nomine utilem Aquiliae habet actionem: directam enim non habet, quoniam dominus membrorum suorum nemo videtur. . . .*

[40] The *actio de effusis vel deiectis.*

[41] D. 9. 3. 7 (Gaius *6 ad ed. prov.*). *Cum liberi hominis corpus ex eo, quod deiectum effusumve quid erit, laesum fuerit, iudex computat mercedes medicis praestitas ceteraque impendia, quae in curatione facta sunt, praeterea operarum, quibus caruit aut cariturus est ob id, quod inutilis factus est. cicatricium autem aut deformitatis nulla fit aestimatio, quia liberorum corpus nullam recipit aestimationem.*

[42] E.g. Grotius, *Inleiding tot de Hollandsche Rechtsgeleertheyd*, 3. 34. 2 (first published at the Hague in 1631); Voet, *Commentarius ad Pandectas*, 9. 2. 11 (first published at the Hague in 1698/1704); Matthaeus, *De Criminibus* (Utrecht, 1644), 47. 3. 4; Groenewegen, *Tractatus de legibus abrogatis et inusitatis in Hollandia vicinisque regionibus*, D. 9. 3. 7 (first published at Leiden, in 1649).

[43] Voet, loc. cit.; Matthaeus, loc. cit.; Groenewegen, loc. cit.

[44] *Commentarii variique resolutiones juris civilis communis et regii*, III, c. 6. n. 12, (first published at Salamanca in 1554–1555).

[45] '*Adde tamen quod in muliere bene aestimaretur praedicta cicatrix et deformitas, saltem quando non est nupta, quia per hoc difficilius et cum maiori dote inveniret maritum, cui nubere possit.*'

was not married', suggests that the rule was being widened and it is not surprising to find that Farinacius,[46] who cites Gomez, gives the action on account of the disfigurement of a woman especially when she is not married (*praesertim non nuptam*) and her dowry has to be greatly increased. Gomez and Farinacius both declare, however, that though no estimate of damages is made of a free man's scar or deformity, the injured party will rate his injury more highly on account of it and an upright judge will give greater damages.[47] Dionysius Gothofredus in his comment on the word *deformitas* in D. 9. 3. 7[48] makes the award of damages apply to women generally, but not to men. The form of his comment is very significant for the history of the rule: 'No estimate of damages is made, as here, for deformity. The more recent jurists accept this in the case of the male; Ravennas and Albericus deny this in the case of the female.' Thus, the refusal of damages is stated as the general principle, and only later does it emerge that the refusal applies only to half of the human race. And the Dutch go further. Matthaeus[49] says disfigurement should be taken into account especially in the case of unmarried women, and Groenewegen[50] declares that the Dutch and French rightly make no distinction between the sexes. Even earlier, Grotius simply said 'Pain and disfigurement of the body, though properly incapable of compensation, are assessed in money, if such is demanded'.[51, 52]

Voluntary major transplants – that is, when either an entire legal system or a large portion of it is moved to a new sphere – fall into three main categories. First when a people moves into a different territory where there is no comparable civilisation, and takes its law with it. Secondly, when a people moves into a different territory where there

---

[46] *Praxis et Theoria criminalium rerum*, lib. 1. tit. 3. quaest. 18, n. 99. This work was first published at Frankfurt in 1597.

[47] Thus, Gomez: '*Verum tamen est, quod eo casu, quo cicatrix, vel deformitas non deberet aestimari in homine libero, tamen offensus gravius aestimabit propter hoc iniuriam, et offensam suam, et similiter probus, et rectus iudex gravius condemnabit, quia ex hoc diceretur atrox iniuria. . . .*'

[48] '*Deformitatis nulla fit aestimatio*, ut hic. *In masculo hoc interpretes admittunt: in foemina vero negant Ravennas Albericus ad l.* 3. 8, 3 *si quadrupes, i. v. t* l § 5. 3 *eod. l.* 106 *inf. de reg.*'

[49] Loc. cit.

[50] Loc. cit.

[51] Loc. cit. 'De smert ende ontciering van't lichaem, hoewel eighentlick niet en zign vergoedelick, werden op geld geschat, soo wanneer sulcks versocht werd.'

[52] Since this is not primarily a work of legal history no attempt is made here to trace the precise steps of this development in detail.

is a comparable civilisation, and takes its law with it. Thirdly, when a people voluntarily accepts a large part of the system of another people or peoples. These three categories should be borne in mind in the instances which follow, though the examples are not chosen on that account and are given principally in historical order.

[Actually, receptions and transplants come in all shapes and sizes. One might think also of an imposed reception, solicited imposition, penetration, infiltration, crypto-reception, inoculation and so on,[53] and it would be perfectly possible to distinguish these and classify them systematically. Again we are faced with a choice. There is, I suggest, no point in elaborating a detailed classification of borrowing until individual instances have been examined to see what they reveal. It is up to those (if any) who would wish to elaborate types of transplantation to show what new light the classification would cast on the data.]

[53] Cf. G. Tedeschi, 'On Reception and on the Legislative Policy of Israel', *Scripta Hierosolymitana*, xvi (Jerusalem, 1966), pp. 11ff, and the works he cites, especially perhaps M. Rheinstein, 'Types of Reception', *Annales de la Faculté de Droit d'Istambul*, vi (1956), pp. 31ff.

CHAPTER 5

ROMANS AND ROMAN LAW IN ROMAN EGYPT

In the ancient Mediterranean world, law was generally personal rather than territorial.[1] Thus in Greco-Roman Egypt, the Egyptians were governed by native Egyptian private law, the Greeks by the Hellenistic 'common law' (legal κοινή), the Romans by Roman law and other smaller groups – such as the Jews – by their personal law. As might be expected, each group of legal rules and customs was influenced by the others, but here we will concern ourselves only with the effects on Roman law.[2] After the Roman conquest of Egypt by Augustus (30 B.C.) the Roman presence was considerable, and consisted in the main of soldiers, civil servants, merchants, and the families of these.

Roman law in Egypt[3] consisted of imperial constitutions, edicts of prefects, *senatusconsulta* and case law. Whether a special *edictum provinciale* of jurisdictional character existed in Egypt is doubtful.[4] It is beyond question, however, that the numerous Imperial constitutions gave even official Roman law in Egypt characteristics differing from the law in Italy.[5] But these we will leave aside, and look only at the unofficial changes – those not sanctioned by Imperial authority but which crept in as a result of contact with other legal systems.

---

[1] But the 'personal law' concept is disputed; cf., e.g., J. Modrzejewski, *Essays in honor of C. B. Welles* (New Haven, 1966), pp. 140ff.

[2] Our knowledge of law in Egypt at this time is mainly derived from papyri concerned with individual cases. This means we have only a very imperfect record, which makes dating of changes almost impossible. We also have to reckon with bad lawyers and plain mistakes.

[3] Cf., e.g., R. Taubenschlag, *The Law of Greco-Roman Egypt in the light of the Papyri*, 2nd edit. (Warsaw, 1955), pp. 27ff; J. Modrzejewski, 'La Règle de droit dans l'Égypte Romaine', *Proceedings of the Twelfth International Congress of Papyrology* (American Studies in Papyrology, 7, Toronto, 1970), pp. 317ff.

[4] Cf. most recently, R. Katzoff, 'The Provincial Edict in Egypt', *T.v.R.* xxxvii (1969), pp. 414ff; R. Martini, *Ricerche in tema di editto provinciale* (Milan, 1966), pp. 129ff, 144ff; Modrzejewski, 'Règle de droit', pp. 341ff; H. Ankum, 'Les Édits des préfets d'Égypte et le problème de l'*edictum provinciale*', *Annales de la Faculté de Droit et des Sciences Économiques de Toulouse*, xviii (1970), pp. 357ff.

[5] Cf., e.g., Taubenschlag, *Law*, pp. 29ff. On the question of 'Reichsrecht' and 'Provinzialrecht' see Modrzejewski, 'Règle de droit', pp. 337ff.

Thus, in the law of persons, the form of marriage is affected by native Egyptian law.[6] More importantly, marriage occurs between brother and sister until the *Constitutio Antoniniana* of A.D. 212[7] though marriage within the fourth degree was prohibited by Roman law. A mother acquired the right to give her daughter in marriage[8] and also to divorce her,[9] whereas in Roman law these powers belonged only to the *paterfamilias*. A Roman father's power over his children (*patria potestas*) which continued so long as he was alive, came in Egypt to be regarded as *tutela*,[10] and it could be created by a local type of adoption[11] and ended by a local ἀποκήρυξις.[12] Romans in Egypt seem to have acquired the Egyptian right of selling their children.[13] Numerous papyri from the early 3rd century on show that a son had legal capacity in property matters,[14] whereas in Roman law everything he acquired belonged to his *paterfamilias*. Guardianship, too, underwent various changes of which the most un-Roman were that a woman could be appointed as guardian,[15] and a foreign guardian might occasionally be appointed to a Roman.[16]

Contrary to Roman law in Italy, Roman slaves seem to be treated as capable of owning property.[17] The formal method of freeing a slave *inter vivos*, *manumissio vindicta*, disappeared in the 3rd century

---

[6] Especially the γάμος ἀγραφος; *P. Oxy.* IV. 973₁₇₋₁₈ (4th century A.D.): Taubenschlag, *Law*, p. 119.

[7] *P. Lond.* III. 936, pp. 30–1 (A.D. 217); Taubenschlag, *Law*, p. 111; Modrzejewski, 'Die Geschwisterehe in der hellenistischen Praxis und nach römischem Recht', *Z.S.S.* lxxxi (1964), pp. 52ff.

[8] E.g. *P. Oxy.* 1273 (A.D. 260); Taubenschlag, *Law*, p. 152.

[9] *P. Cair. Preis.* No. 2 (A.D. 362); Taubenschlag, loc. cit.

[10] E.g. *B.G.U.* 667 (A.D. 221–222); *S.B.* 1010 (A.D. 299); Taubenschlag, *Law*, p. 132.

[11] *P. Lips.* 28 (4th century A.D.); *P. Oxy.* 1206 (A.D. 335); Taubenschlag, *Law*, p. 135.

[12] *P. Oxy.* 1206₁₃₋₁₄ (probably late 2nd century A.D.); Modrzejewski, 'Règle de droit', p. 363.

[13] *P. Lips.* 35₁₇ (4th century A.D.); *P. Oxy.* 1206₁₁ (A.D. 335), Taubenschlag, *Law*, p. 139.

[14] E.g. *P. Grenf.* 49 (A.D. 220); *B.G.U.* 667 (A.D. 221–222); *P. Oxy.* 1040 (A.D. 225); Taubenschlag, *Law*, pp. 146f.

[15] *Mich. Inv.* no. 2922 (A.D. 172–173)=*SB* 7538; *P. Lond.* III. 1164a (A.D. 212); *B.G.U.* 888 (A.D. 159–160); Taubenschlag, *Law*, p. 159. The right of a woman to be *tutor* was accepted by Imperial law in A.D. 390; *C.Th.* 3. 17. 3: Modrzejewski, 'Règle de droit', p. 361.

[16] *Mich. Inv.* no. 2922; Taubenschlag, *Law*, p. 158.

[17] *P. Oxy.* 244₁₅ (A.D. 23); Taubenschlag, *Law*, p. 89.

A.D. to be replaced by the local method of freeing before a notary public.[18]

In the law of contract, Greek forms and terminology become common.[19] The Egyptians recognised direct representation in receipts of payments from the late 2nd century B.C.[20] and in purchases from at least the early 2nd century A.D.[21] The Romans in Egypt accepted direct agency in situations such as leases,[22] loans,[23] receipts,[24] sales[25] and stipulations;[26] all this despite the failure of metropolitan Roman law to develop any principle of agency. The standard Roman contract of sale, *emptio venditio*, was consensual, and transfer of ownership under it was separate and required physical delivery, *traditio*, of the object. But the Romans in Egypt accepted the local καταγραφή[27] which was apparently both a formal written contract (drawn up by a public official) and a conveyance. Again, in Roman law a contract to benefit third parties was void and could not be enforced even by the contracting parties, but in Egypt Romans make leases in which the rent is to be paid to an outside body.[28]

In succession, Greek forms of clauses are used in wills, and an executor (unknown to Roman law) makes his appearance.[29] There are

---

[18] *B.G.U.* 96 (3rd century A.D.); Taubenschlag, *Law*, p. 99; Modrzejewski, 'Règle de droit', pp. 360f, and the references he gives, p. 361, n. 276.

[19] On what follows see H. J. Wolff, 'Zur Romanisierung des Vertragsrechts der Papyri', *Z.S.S.* lxx (1956), pp. 1ff.

[20] *P. Rein.* 11₃ (III B.C.): Taubenschlag, *Law*, p. 308.

[21] Papyrus from A.D. 116 quoted by Taubenschlag, *Law*, p. 308, n. 2.

[22] E.g. *P. Théad.* 8 (A.D. 306); *P. Lips.* 19 (A.D. 319–320); *P. Gen.* 66 (A.D. 374); Taubenschlag, *Law*, p. 311.

[23] E.g. *P. Lond.* II. 429, p. 314 (A.D. 350); *P. Amh.* 147 (5th–6th century A.D); Taubenschlag, loc. cit.

[24] E.g. *B.G.U.* 1662₁₇ (A.D. 182); *P. Flor.* 75 (A.D. 380); Taubenschlag, loc. cit.

[25] E.g. *P. Rainer* 25. 817 (A.D. 189); *C.P.R.* I, 8 (A.D. 218); 1634 (A.D. 222); Taubenschlag, loc. cit.

[26] *P. Lond.* III. 954₂₀ p. 153; Taubenschlag, p. 312.

[27] *P. Gr. Vindob.* 19. 853 (A.D. 319); cf. Modrzejewski, 'Règle de droit', p. 339, n. 145.

[28] *P.S.I.* 241 (3rd century A.D.); *P. Strassb.* 2 (A.D. 217): Taubenschlag, *Law*, p. 402.

[29] Cf. Will of Longinus Castor: *B.G.U.* 326; Taubenschlag, *Law*, pp. 195, 198. On other aspects of this will see A. Watson, *Irish Jurist*, i (1966), pp. 313ff. On Roman wills in Egypt in general see M. Amelotti, *Il testamento romano attraverso la prassi documentale*, i (Florence, 1966), and Modrzejewski, 'Règle de droit', p. 361, n. 284.

also a few changes in the law of property: for instance, a right of way is treated merely as an obligation.[30]

Thus, Roman law as practised in Egypt underwent vast changes, especially in the law of persons and contract, as a result of the experience of foreign systems. Three important preliminary conclusions can be drawn from this incomplete and superficial survey.

In the first place, it has been shown that it is not necessarily the case that family law is the branch of law least open to foreign influence.[31] Roman family law was extremely conservative and static – as often family law elsewhere – and sometimes the changes which did occur in it were due to juristic interpretation[32] rather than legislation[33] or edict. In Egypt Roman traditions of law were not so strong, and large sections of the Roman population were very willing to jettison some of the most Roman parts – e.g. incidents of *patria potestas*.

In the second place, gaps or deficiencies in a legal system are seen to be not always due to lack of knowledge that there is a deficiency. The illogicality of legal development is also highlighted. Thus, there would be little disagreement among modern lawyers that direct representation is of considerable advantage to a society. Yet once it was recognised by the Romans in Egypt the concept could not fail to become known to the metropolitan Roman jurists. But Roman law never accepted agency or direct representation.[34] Again, the jurists at Rome never recognised (as a general rule) that a *filiusfamilias* might be capable of owning property. The obvious conclusion which we have drawn from this is of significance even apart from any question of transplants or of Comparative Law. The lesson is important especially for historians trying to reconstruct the past on a basis of common sense and logic, in the absence of concrete evidence. Thus, the important and famous Roman *actio Publiciana* is usually dated to 67 B.C., but there is not the slightest indication of its existence for another century and a half. The main reasons for preferring the early date are that 67 B.C. when one of the praetors was called Publicius would fit the general course of development of Roman law,[35] and that there was an important

30 *P. Gen.* 11 (A.D. 350); Taubenschlag, *Law*, p. 259.
31 Cf. infra, p. 97.
32 E.g. the virtual disappearance of marriage *cum manu*.
33 Though Augustus's legislation was responsible for much change.
34 Of course, functionally the Romans had means which achieved much of the advantages of direct representation. But apart even from the conceptual deficiency, there were also practical limitations in what was available.
35 Especially by the Edict.

gap in the law for the action to fill.[36] This opinion may be correct, but its basis is clearly fragile.[37] Publicius, after all, was not an uncommon name.

In the third place, legal rules which are unsatisfactory at home appear even less satisfactory when they are transplanted. Jeremy Bentham in the fourth chapter of his work, *Of the Influence of Time and Place in Matters of Legislation*, said '. . . I would venture to lay down the following propositions: 1st, That the English law is a great part of it of such a nature, as to be bad everywhere: 2nd, But that it would not only be, but appear worse in Bengal than in England: 3rd, That a system might be devised, which, while it would be better for Bengal, would also be better, even for England.'[38] Hence a time of transplant is often a moment when reforms can be introduced.

[36] Cf. most recently, M. Kaser, *T.v.R.* xxxvii (1969), pp. 585f.

[37] Cf. A. Watson, *The Law of Property in the Later Roman Republic* (Oxford, 1969), pp. 104ff.

[38] For English law in India, see A. Gledhill, 'The Reception of English Law in India', in W. B. Hamilton (ed.), *The Transfer of Institutions* (Durham, N.C., 1964), pp. 165ff.

CHAPTER 6

ROMAN SYSTEMATICS IN SCOTLAND

The reception of Roman law in Scotland has been an extremely slow process. Its origins can be traced back to the 12th century, and some rules have been accepted only this century. It might be a mistake to think that the reception is even now at an end.

The influence of Roman law in Scots law has been both on positive rules and on systematisation. The latter we will look at first, partly because the history is more straightforward but mainly because the adoption of another's systematics probably has more far-reaching yet less obvious consequences than the adoption of individual rules, no matter how numerous these are.

The most important and influential law book the world has ever known is Justinian's *Institutes*. This work, issued in A.D. 533 as a students' elementary textbook but having the force of law, is still required reading for beginners in law in many of the world's universities. More especially it was the basis of beginners' legal study in European law schools in the Middle Ages and Renaissance. It is divided into four books. The first deals with the nature of law, sources of law, and the law of persons. The second with the classification of things including incorporeal rights, the law of property and testate succession. Book three deals with intestate succession, obligations (in general), contracts and quasi-contracts. Book four with delict, quasi-delict, actions and, in one final short section, criminal law.[1] The only branches of law dealt with in the *Institutes* which are totally different from the law prevailing in Scotland are actions and crimes.

The earliest known Scottish legal treatise is the *Regiam Majestatem* probably of the 14th century, and about two-thirds of it is derived from the English work attributed to Glanvill, *Tractatus de legibus et consuetudinibus regni Angliae*. But the unknown author of the *Regiam* probably had direct knowledge of Justinian's *Institutes*. As P. G. Stein has recently pointed out, 'whereas Justinian begins *imperatoriam maiestatem* and Glanvill has *regiam potestatem*, the Scottish writer achieves the

---

[1] This arrangement itself is in general not original to Justinian but goes back (at least) to the *Institutes* of Gaius in the 2nd century A.D.

compromise opening *regiam maiestatem*'.[2] One may also see the influence, direct or indirect, of Justinian's *Institutes* in that the *Regiam Majestatem* is divided into 4 books, whereas Glanvill has 14. But the further arrangement within each book can only to a very limited degree be regarded as descending from Justinian. Thus, book one is concerned with courts, procedure and pacts; book two with arbitration, serfs and bondsmen, dowry, succession and feudal tenure; book three with contractual obligations and procedure; and book four with crimes. The influence of Glanvill on the form is more immediate than that of Justinian.

Little system is to be observed in the works of the following centuries until Hope's *Major Practicks* in the early 17th century.[3] This also is in four books: (i) Law and Government, Civil and Ecclesiastical; (ii) Personal Rights; (iii) Real Rights; (iv) Wills and Succession. The arrangement is obviously neat. Then in 1681 was published the first edition of Stair's *Institutions of the Law of Scotland*[4] which is regarded as the foundation of the modern law of Scotland. This work too is in four books, and the general order of topics is slightly closer to Justinian. Book one deals with the common principles of law, law of persons, delict, and contract; book two with the law of property; book three mainly with succession; and book four with procedure. Even the most cursory glance over the titles into which the work is divided shows, however, that the order of topics differs considerably from that of Justinian and also that, as in the *Regiam Majestatem* and Hope's *Major Practicks*, many aspects of law are discussed which are very remote from any possible counterpart in the Roman work.

But three years later, in 1684, the Lord Advocate, Sir George Mackenzie, published his tiny *Institutions of the Law of Scotland* for which he claims to have treated nothing save Terms and Principles. Again the work is in four parts: Part one discusses laws in general, the courts and the law of persons; Part two the law of things and property; Part three obligations in general, contracts and intestate succession; Part four actions and crimes. Thus, Part one follows closely

---

[2] *Roman Law in Scotland*, part 5, 13b of *Ius romanum medii aevi* (Milan, 1968), p. 15. It is possible that the author of *Regiam* did not have direct knowledge of Justinian's *Institutes*, but of another intermediary. The phrase *regia maiestas* was used in France as a mode of address by 1238: cf. now Lord Cooper, *Regiam Majestatem* (Stair Society, Edinburgh, 1947), p. 59.

[3] The organisation of material should be contrasted with that in Balfour's *Practicks* which appear to date from 1579.

[4] The work is in manuscript from about 1665 on.

Justinian book one. Part two follows book two apart from its omission of testate succession which did not really exist in Scotland for heritable property until 31st December 1868. Part three inverts obligations and intestate succession (not surprisingly perhaps since in Justinian intestate succession comes where it does as following upon testate succession). Part four follows Justinian except for the omission of delict.

Mackenzie's arrangement was expressly followed by John Erskine in his *Institute of the Law of Scotland* which was first published in 1773. Every title of Mackenzie's book is matched by one in Erskine.

There is, though, a vital distinction between the *Institutions* of Mackenzie and the *Institute* of Erskine. The former, which is rather shorter than Justinian's *Institutes*, is only about one-twentieth of the length of Erskine. Erskine, in other words, is concerned not only with the terms and principles of the law but also with its details. This is a matter of some significance. Scotland, a country with (fortunately) a relatively simple system of law which is not overburdened with cases, has tended to rely quite heavily on the authority of its jurists who have written a comprehensive treatise on the whole law. Thus, in the 17th century Stair (whose *Institutions* are approximately of the same length as Erskine's *Institute*), in the 18th century Erskine, and in the 19th century Bell were the 'Institutional writers' *par excellence*. The concept of a single comprehensive book on the whole law, fundamental for student and practitioner alike, still flourishes in Scotland in the 20th century: Gloag and Henderson, *Introduction to the Law of Scotland*, 1st edit. (Edinburgh, 1927), now in its 7th edition (Edinburgh, 1968) by A. M. Johnston and J. A. D. Hope; T. B. Smith, *A Short Commentary on the Law of Scotland* (Edinburgh, 1962); D. M. Walker, *Principles of Scottish Private Law* (Oxford, 1970). Of this last the publishers can reasonably say on the end-paper: 'This book is a completely new, systematic and comprehensive statement of the whole of the substantive private law of Scotland . . .' Works of this kind could not be contemplated in England or in the United States.

With Erskine then, the arrangement of Justinian's elementary textbook for students became important for the organisation of law in Scotland.

This Romanisation of the systematics of Scots law suffered a setback in the 19th century with George Joseph Bell, the third celebrated Institutional writer. His *Principles of the Law of Scotland* was first published in 1829 and was arranged in five – not four – books. Book First covered contract, Book Second property; Book Third persons and succession; Book Fourth status; and Book Fifth procedure. The order has been much altered from Justinian's *Institutes*. More important, though, is a change in emphasis: the new stress on shipping law and even on feudal land law is thoroughly un-Roman. It is well known that Bell's work was much influenced by English law. The days of Romanisation seemed to have passed.

But this century has seen a resurgence of Roman law influence on the systematics. The most influential general book of the 20th century to date is Gloag and Henderson's *Introduction* which has already been mentioned. It is divided into chapters and not into books and the order is by no means that of Justinian. But the subcutaneous influence of Roman law can be seen in the marked decline of the space attributed to the non-Roman elements. Thus, of the total of 775 pages of text, feudal landownership has 30, and company law only 29. More significant in this respect is Smith's *Short Commentary*. Part three, that on Private law, has the order: General legal concepts, family law, succession, law of property, trusts, obligations. How much this owes, consciously or unconsciously, to Justinian's *Institutes* is plain.[5] And the non-Roman elements, such as company law, modern social legislation, are excluded from consideration. On the arrangement of Walker's *Principles*, the Justinianian influence is also obvious, though it is not so marked.

But the clearest indication of the influence of the Roman system in the present century has been in the organisation of the University courses. Thus to take an example from a particular time and University,[6] at Edinburgh, there were twenty Ordinary Law courses in the academic year 1970/71.

1 Civil Law (i.e. primarily Roman Law)
2 Criminal Law
3 Constitutional Law
4 Scots Law I
5 Scots Law II
6 Jurisprudence
7 Mercantile Law
8 Conveyancing

[5] Smith himself says that his order of arrangement is based on Stair: *M.L.R.* xxvi (1963), p. 608. But it is closer to Justinian.

[6] There have been frequent changes in the syllabuses, but the pattern found in this instance has been typical of the Universities of Glasgow, Aberdeen and Edinburgh.

    9 Forensic Medicine
    10 Evidence and Procedure
    11 Administrative Law
    12 Accounting
    13 Taxation
    14 Agricultural Law
    15 Public International Law
    16 Comparative Constitutions
    17 International Private Law
    18 International Organisations
    19 Criminology
    20 Comparative Law

Some of these, of course, cannot be considered important in this connection. But it should be noticed that 'Scots Law' is not regarded as including 'Criminal Law', 'Constitutional Law', 'Mercantile Law', 'Conveyancing', 'Evidence and Procedure', and so on. All the non-Roman elements are treated as falling outside 'Scots Law'.[7] The syllabuses of the Scots Law classes are:

Scots Law I

History and sources;
machinery of justice;
general legal concepts;
family law;
legal rights;
intestate succession.

Scots Law II

Testate succession;
administration of estates;
property;
trusts;
obligations (comprising voluntary and delictual obligations, un-justified enrichment, and *negotiorum gestio*).[8]

The arrangement is again very much that of Justinian's *Institutes*. This exclusive nature of the Scots law course is, it must be emphasised,

    [7] *Mutatis mutandis*, this is also true of Continental codes.
    [8] For all this see *Edinburgh University Calendar*, 1970–71 (Edinburgh, 1970), pp. 256ff.

a 20th-century phenomenon, and is not found, for instance, in Baron Hume's lectures, the most famous 19th-century course.[9]

The systematisation of modern civil law on the basis of Justinian's *Institutes* is, of course, not confined to Scots law.[10] The same systematisation can be found, to a greater or lesser extent, in all the modern civil codes which derive from Roman law. Thus, the Dutch civil code (*Burgerlijk Wetboek*) is divided into four books: the first deals with persons, the second with things (including succession), the third with obligations, the fourth with proof and prescription.[11] The arrangement is rather neater, though at the expense of making book four very much shorter than the others. The contents are fundamentally the same as those of the *Institutes* with the omission of procedure – Roman procedure is, of course, remote from modern – and the insertion of the contents of book 4. The Spanish civil code (*Código civil*) is also in four books: book one is persons, two is things, ownership and rights less than ownership, three is the various ways of acquiring ownership (includes and is mainly succession), four is obligations and contracts. This again is very much the *Institutes* with the omission of procedure. Other civil codes may have more or fewer books than four but the influence of Justinian is clear. (This is least apparent in the German *Bürgerliches Gesetzbuch* which has a more intellectual arrangement than the others.)

This organisation in modern civil law systems is very obvious to the outsider. J. H. Merryman, for instance, points out that the first three books of Justinian's *Institutes* and the major 19th-century civil codes 'all deal with substantially the same set of problems and relationships and the substantive area they cover is what a civil lawyer calls "civil law" '.[12] Yet the legal rules themselves have changed since 533.

Systematisation, of course, has effects.[13] Thus, in Scotland, one has to point out that the basic law books used by students and practitioners

[9] The lectures are to be found published by the Stair Society, as volumes 5, 13, 15, 17, 18, 19 (Edinburgh, 1939, 1949, 1952, 1955, 1957 and 1958), and edited by G. C. H. Paton.

[10] Thus, A. H. Campbell rightly claims: 'No other book has contributed so much to the structure of modern jurisprudence': *The Structure of Stair's Institutions* (Glasgow University Publications, xcviii; Glasgow, 1954), p. 9.

[11] The *Burgerlijk Wetboek* is in course of being replaced, and some parts of the new *Ontwerp* are now in force.

[12] *The Civil Law Tradition* (Stanford, 1969), p. 7; cf. also p. 73.

[13] As has classification.

alike underestimate the practical legal significance of the non-Roman elements in law – company law for instance, welfare legislation, tax and so on. This has undoubtedly contributed to the fact that practising Scottish lawyers have traditionally seen their function in a more restricted way than do their American counterparts; that Scottish law students are less interested in immediate social problems than are American students – of course, Scotland also does not have such pressing problems. The students' attitude as to what is *real* law, what law really matters, is also influenced by the fact that part of the curriculum is labelled *Scots* law, and that other parts have merely specific labels like mercantile law, agricultural law, conveyancing and evidence. Indeed at Edinburgh in 1970/71 Scots law was compulsory whereas the others just mentioned were options. There is something strange in this. Why should the law of husband and wife, guardianship, parent and child, be compulsory objects of study for all students when company law and taxation are not? Most Scottish lawyers, both solicitors and advocates, will pass their whole working career without once touching a problem of parent and child apart from questions of custody on divorce. Divorce is common, and divorce cases form a large part of lawyers' work,[14] but difficult legal problems in divorce are most unusual. A knowledge of company law on the other hand is of great practical importance; and in Scotland, in marked contrast to the United States, lawyers have usually been unable to give proper advice on the tax implications of legal transactions.[15] But family law is traditionally part of the legal system: company law and taxation are not. Thus the same attitude is apparent inside law schools and in practice.

In European countries, the civil code is always regarded as the basic law – it is on this that most attention is focussed – and the other codes are to some extent treated as secondary. Merryman, in fact, declares that one of the principal distinguishing marks of what common lawyers call the civil law system is the belief that the subjects treated in these codes form 'a related body of law that constitutes the fundamental content of the legal system'.[16] The real law, which most inter-

---

[14] Especially of advocates. Even undefended divorce actions must be heard in the Court of Session, and not in any lower court.

[15] But the situation in Scotland is gradually changing.

[16] *Tradition*, p. 7. On p. 73 he says, 'Civil law is still fundamental law. It is studied first, and subsequent study builds on it. It forms the matrix of thought of the lawyer in the civil law tradition.'

ests academics and practitioners alike, is that which has derived from Roman law as set out in Justinian's *Institutes*. This influence of Roman law is not less significant but more significant because it is largely unnoticed: Dutch practitioners are not usually conscious of the origins of the content of the *Burgerlijk Wetboek*; neither do Scots students or teachers reflect on the restricted content of the Scots law course.

CHAPTER 7

THE RECEPTION OF ROMAN LAW
IN SCOTLAND

On the substance of Scots law, Roman influence is apparent from the time of the earliest sources and has continued, in one form or another, even up to the present day.[1]

Thus, though we do not have early customary burgh laws for any particular burgh we have a collection in 119 chapters, the *Leges Quatuor Burgorum*, which seem in fact to have applied more widely than to the four burghs of Edinburgh, Stirling, Roxburgh and Berwick. The first 21 chapters go back to the reign of David I (b. 1084, d. 1153), and the remainder seem to date from 1150–1250. There is little in the customary provisions which can be regarded as showing the influence of Roman law but there is an indication here and there.[2] Similarities in the language are not necessarily significant, but chapter 28 permits a burgess to put a decisory oath to a defendant who denies the debt. Chapter 118 is particularly interesting. A husband, it says, is liable for his wife's delicts against a neighbour, and he must punish her when she acts negligently without the husband's advice, *sicut puerum infra aetatem castigare cum non sit sui iuris*. In this, *cum non sit sui iuris* seems to refer to the Roman father's *patria potestas*, a power which continued so long as the *pater* remained alive, but *infra aetatem* reveals that in Scotland the father's authority to punish ended when the child reached

---

[1] It may be observed that what is possibly the earliest reported case from Scotland is itself Roman: D. 49. 15. 6 (Pomponius *1 ex var. lect.*). A woman sentenced to toil in salt works on account of a crime she had committed was carried off by robbers belonging to a tribe outside the Empire. She was sold *iure commercii* and then redeemed. The jurist Pomponius of the 2nd century A.D. held that she was restored to her previous condition, and the price paid for her was to be given from the treasury to the centurion, Cocceius Firmus. The Antonine wall in Scotland between the Forth and Clyde more or less marked the boundary of Empire, salt pans were worked in the Forth (at least in later times) and a centurion, Marcus Cocceius Firmus of the 2nd legion, dedicated 5 altars at Auchendavy camp on the wall.

[2] Cf., e.g., D. Baird Smith in *The Sources and Literature of Scots Law* (The Stair Society, vol. 1, Edinburgh, 1936), pp. 171ff; P. G. Stein, *Roman Law in Scotland*, part 5, 13b of *Ius romanum medii aevi* (Milan, 1968), p. 9.

a certain age. This semi-adoption of Roman law has always been typical of Scotland.

The rather later costumal of Perth contains the earliest references to 'the learned law of the continent' and parts derive from Ivo of Chartres and Isidorus.[3] Other works, especially the influential *liber de iudiciis*, show a growing awareness of Continental legal scholarship, and that some Roman law was creeping in primarily as a result of the acceptance of rules of romano-canonical procedure. The most important Scottish mediaeval law book is the *Regiam Majestatem* of which as already mentioned about two-thirds derive from the English jurist Glanvill who died in 1190. It seems reasonable to suppose that the reason he, and not his later compatriot Bracton, was used was because in the 13th century Scottish and English common law began to go separate ways: England to have numerous forms of process, each with a narrow precise scope, Scotland to have a few actions each with a much wider field of application.[4] But the *Regiam* also contains sections showing the influence of Roman law and canon law: on pacts and unilateral promises, pacts *in rem* and pacts *in personam*, pacts valid and invalid, which persons are bound by pacts;[5] arbiters and arbitration;[6] ordination and manumission of serfs;[7] and gifts between husband and wife.[8] Stein has convincingly shown[9] that the source of these sections is Goffredus de Trano's *Summa in titulos decretalium* which was written between 1241 and 1246. Thus, as one might expect, Roman law coming into Scotland at this time did so through the medium of Canon law.

All this so far has been on book production. But in litigation[10] – especially that involving religious bodies, much of which was referred to Rome – we find traces of Roman law: *longissimi temporis praescriptio, longa praescriptione iusto titulo et bona fide, restitutio in integrum, laesio enormis*. The references are at times rather vague. Renunciation of the right to specific remedies was common in contracts in Germany and the Low Countries and the same practice is found in Scotland from the

[3] Cf. Stein, *Roman Law*, pp. 10ff.
[4] Cf. Stein, *Roman Law*, pp. 21ff.
[5] Book I, 28–31.
[6] Book II, 1–10.
[7] Book II, 13–14.
[8] Book II, 15.
[9] 'The source of the Romano-canonical part of *Regiam Maiestatem*', *Scottish Historical Review*, xlviii (1969), pp. 107ff.
[10] Cf. Stein, *Roman Law*, pp. 22ff.

middle of the 13th century: *exceptio doli, beneficium restitutionis in integrum, remedium epistolae divi Hadriani, condictio ex lege, condictio sine causa, condictio iniusta causa, senatus consultum Velleianum, lex Julia de fundo dotali, exceptio non numeratae pecuniae.* The impression left by these renunciations – and by their prominence – is that the parties feared the agreement might be later set aside at the instance of one of them by the skill of a lawyer learned in Roman law. The conclusion cannot be avoided that Roman law might successfully be adduced as a latent source of law in Scotland at that time, and as covering these agreements. Much of the debate in the Great Cause of Scotland (i.e. the debate on the succession to the Throne which began in 1291) also related to Roman law. 14th-century litigation shows the continuing advance of Roman law.

The break with England after the War of Independence[11] and the absence of any University in Scotland led to Scots going to Europe to study. We know of the careers of more than 400 Scottish students for the seventy years before 1410 (the date of foundation of the oldest Scottish University, the University of St. Andrews, is 1413). Most of them studied in France and 120 of the 230 whose faculty is known studied law, and a further 80 went on to a Law Faculty after finishing in Arts.[12] All of these students would learn a considerable amount of Civil Law even though the majority specialised in Canon Law (itself heavily influenced by Civil Law). The Scottish Universities, once founded, for a long time were not generally successful in teaching law and the Scots continued to study abroad: mainly in Cologne, Louvain and North Italy in the 15th century, France in the 16th century until the Reformation, and thereafter in Holland. Thus, between 1600 and 1800 about 1600 Scotsmen matriculated in the Law Faculty at Leiden alone.[13]

The place Roman law had won in early 17th-century Scotland is well illustrated by introductory remarks of two writers. Thomas Craig who died in 1608 writes in his *Ius Feudale*:[14] 'But we in this

[11] Scotland's independence was recognised by the English king in 1328 by the Treaty of Northampton.

[12] Cf. Stein, *Roman Law*, pp. 40f, following the unpublished Oxford thesis of Dr. D. E. R. Watt.

[13] J. C. Gardner in *Sources and Literature*, pp. 232f, relying on evidence provided by E. M. Meijers.

[14] '*Nos tamen in hoc qualicunque regno Romanorum legibus ita obligamur, quatenus legibus naturae et recte rationi congruent: . . . apud nos scriptarum legum maxima inopia et naturaliter in plerisque negotiis jus Civile sequimur. Non quidem edocti, et*

kingdom are bound by the laws of the Romans in so far as they are in
harmony with the laws of nature and right reason. . . . Here there
is an extreme scarcity of written laws and naturally we follow the
Civil Law in most matters. Not indeed that we are learned and trained
in that law, because until now so far as I am aware there have been no
professors of law who taught law publicly – which is, of course, to
be regretted – but almost against our will since we lack our own
written law, led only by the kindness of nature, or the dignity of that
system of law.' Thus Roman law is used when it accords with the laws
of nature and right reason. Scots written law is very scanty so it is
natural that Civil law is followed in most fields. Very significant for us,
though, is the frank admission that the Scots are not too learned in the
Roman law. Vastly different from Craig's systematic treatise were
the books of 'practicks' which a few judges and advocates compiled
primarily to give the substance of the most important judicial decisions.
Sir Thomas Hope's *Major Practicks* (1605–1633)[15] also acknowledges
the importance of Roman law: 'Nota the act of parliament 1493 c.51
allowes directlie the constitutions of the civil and cannon law in this
realme, his verbis: – since it is permitted be the constitutions and
ordinances of lawes civill and cannon that minors may revock alien-
ations etc. maid to their prejudice in their minoritie etc., heirfoir
We James be the grace of God King of Scotts revock, reduces etc.;
and so followes his revocatione. ITEM, the act 1425 c.48 (bearing the
king's subjects be governed be the lawes of the realme allanerlie)
intends not to exclud the civil and canon law wher we have no municipall statuts, bot allanerlie to excluid the particular lawes maid or
obserued in any shereiffdom or quarter of the cuntrie in prejudice of
the comon law of the realme; as is mair cleir be the act 1503 c.79
quhilk prohibits such lawes speciallie in the Isles, because apparantlie
to that tyme they had reteined the lawes of Denmark to quhom they
perteined of befoir. ITEM, in 1540 c.69, ther being sumonds of tresone
persewit at the king's instance againes the airs of one Robert Leslie, to
heir and sie him forfauted for cryms of treasone committed befoir his
deceis, it wes murmured as ane noveltie that a dead man should be

---

*in eo instituti, quod nulli adhuc, quod sciam, apud nos iuris fuerant professores, qui ius
publice docerent (quod sane dolendum est) sed prope nolentes cum proprio iure scripto
destituamur, sola naturae benignitate aut ipsius iuris dignitate inducti*': Book I, tit. 2 § 8.
The *Ius Feudale* was not published until 1655. Cf. also John Lesley, *De origine,
Moribus, et rebus gestis Scotorum* (Rome, 1578), p. 75.

[15] Printed by *The Stair Society* as volumes 3 and 4 (Edinburgh, 1937, 1938).

accuised. The summonds wes founded upon the comon (or civill) law; and the estaits, being consulted, fand and concluded that the king had good reasone to persew that summonds and all wther sumondiss of treasone conform to the comon law, good equity, and reasone, albeit ther wes na municipall law maid therupon of befoir. Quherby it is cleir that the comon law hes ever had place in this realme notwithstanding of the twa statuts abone written. ITEM, in 1540 c.80, fals nottars and wthers makers and users of falsett ar ordained to be punished efter the disposition of the comon law baith cannon and civill; ergo etc. ITEM, in 1540 c.104, judges ar prohibit to take any budds further then is permitted of the law quhilk is meanit of the civill and comon law. ITEM, fals nottars to be punished as falsaries of the law: 1540 c.80. ITEM, reversiones containeing taylyied gold and silver may be fullfilled be peyment of mony current of the lyke value conforme to the comon law: 1555 c.37. ITEM, the act 1567 c.31 – anent abrogateing of all acts contrarie to the religion – abrogatts and annulls all acts and constitutions, canon civill or municipall, with all wther constitutions and practique introduced against the proffessors thereof. Repeited 1587 c.23.'[16] Hope is concerned to stress another point, namely that the authority of Roman law is acknowledged even by Royal statute.[17]

The most significant event in Scottish legal development was the publication in 1681 of Stair's majestic *Institutions of the Law of Scotland*. This single work, once and for all, made Scots law into a viable system, and is properly regarded as the true foundation of modern Scots law. The influence of Roman law is apparent throughout – direct citation from the sources is, indeed, frequent – and of its place in Scotland he says,[18] 'though it be not acknowledged as a law binding for its authority, yet being, as a rule, followed for its equity'. In this context though, 'as a rule' does not have the sense of 'generally', but means something like 'as a code of conduct'. This is shown by the balance in the sentence of 'as a law binding for its authority' and 'as a rule, followed for its equity'. Moreover, the meaning of 'generally' for 'as a rule' is not evidenced before 1842.[19]

---

[16] Book I, tit. 1 § 14.

[17] It is extremely doubtful whether any of the statutes in question allowed directly the constitutions of Roman or Canon Law in Scotland. But this only makes Hope's attitude more interesting.

[18] I. 1. 12.

[19] Cf. *Oxford English Dictionary*, viii (Oxford, 1933), p. 883.

MacKenzie, whose *Institutions* have already been mentioned, was also an enthusiastic Romanist, and, as the arrangement of the *Institutions* might suggest, a Humanist. In his inaugural lecture as Dean of the Faculty of Advocates he commends the methods of study of the great French Humanist lawyers and says in a much quoted sentence: 'I love equally ill to hear Civil Law spoke to in the terms of a Stile Book or accidental Latin (as is most ordinary) as to hear the genuin words of our Municipal Law forced to express the phrases of the Civil Law and Doctors.'[20] This purist view – at variance with the traditional Scottish approach – gained ground in the following century and lawyers were more diffident in using Roman law out of context.[21]

In the 19th century the industrialisation of society coupled with the great development of English law led the Scots to look to the law of that system rather than to Rome. But even in this present century Roman law continues to exert its influence. The most famous case is *Cantiere San Rocco S.A.* v. *The Clyde Shipbuilding and Engineering Co. Ltd.*[22] An Austrian company ordered machinery from a Scottish firm and paid an instalment of the price. Following upon the outbreak of war performance of the contract became illegal. At the end of the war the Austrian company sued for recovery of the instalment paid and was successful on the basis of the Roman remedy of *condictio causa data causa non secuta*. It may be observed that in general English law gives no remedy for unjustified enrichment.[23] In 1970 argument was led in the Court of Session on a point of interpretation by counsel who adduced in support the famous *causa Curiana* of 93–91 B.C.[24] Scotland is not alone in continuing to be influenced by Roman law. In South Africa the reliance on Roman authority is much more marked.[25] Proposals put forward for the new Dutch divorce law by a committee of humanist lawyers were consciously influenced by classical Roman law. The chairman in fact published on it a newspaper article entitled 'The Romans Didn't Do It So Madly'.[26]

[20] 'What Eloquence is fit for the Bar', in *Pleadings in Some Remarkable Cases* (Edinburgh, 1673), p. 17.
[21] For more detail see P. G. Stein, 'The Influence of Roman Law on the Law of Scotland', *Juridical Review*, viii, N.S. (1963), pp. 205ff.
[22] 1923 S.C. (H.L.) 105.
[23] Though see *Fibrosa Spolka Akeyjna* v. *Fairbairn Lawson Combe Barbour, Ltd.*, [1943] A.C. 32.
[24] Carruthers and Others.   [25] See infra, p. 78 and n. 2.
[26] J. A. Ankum, 'De Romeinen deden het zo gek nog niet', *De Groene Amsterdammer*, 2nd August 1969.

Scots law has the Roman distinction of pupils – males under 14, females under 12 – and minors. Pupils have tutors whose appointment and powers are very similar to those of Roman law, and minors have curators. The modes of transfer of moveable property are almost wholly Roman, and the influence of that system on real security, servitudes, usufruct and succession to moveables is very apparent. But the greatest influence of Roman law is on obligations: on particular contracts, especially on sale, on quasi contract such as unjustified enrichment and *negotiorum gestio*, and on delict.

Craig's lament of the Scots lawyer's ignorance of Roman law has already been stressed. Jurists of later centuries were not necessarily more accurate but this ignorance (or misunderstanding) was not necessarily fatal to the use of Roman law. One instance will be enough here.[27] In the 19th century the transfer of ownership generally required the delivery of the thing to the transferee, the Roman rule. Bell, the leading academic lawyer, declared there was 'another case of necessity, which seems to give sanction to constructive delivery: viz, where goods are purchased from a manufacturer before some necessary operation of his art is completed'.[28] After some elaboration of the rule he notes, 'If we seek for authority for this doctrine in the civil law, we shall find it.' But the texts he gives in support[29] do not concern constructive delivery of goods sold while work has still to be done on them by the seller – indeed, Roman law did not recognise delivery in such circumstances – but what is called *constitutum possessorium*; that is, where it is arranged that ownership is to be transferred but the transferor is to remain in possession under some other title, for instance where the seller hires back the property sold.[30] Oddly, Bell does not accept *constitutum possessorium* as transferring ownership.[31]

I have dealt at considerable length on the reception of Roman law in Scotland because it illustrates several interesting points.

First, it shows how much legal relationships and transplants may owe

---

[27] But see also, e.g., *Faculty Decision* (Kames), no. 126 [Petition of David Malloch, 18th November 1751].

[28] *Commentaries on the Law of Scotland*, i, 7th edit. (Edinburgh, 1870), pp. 187f.

[29] *Commentaries*, i, p. 188, n. 2. The texts relied on are C. 8. 53(54). 28; [A.D. 417] D. 6. 1. 77 (Ulpian *17 ad ed.*)

[30] See the splendidly harsh criticism of Bell by G. Brodie in his (4th) edition of Stair's *Institutions* (Edinburgh, 1826), note on pp. 905f.

[31] But probably Hume would; *Baron Hume's Lectures 1786–1822*, edited by G. C. H. Paton, iii (Edinburgh, 1952), pp. 251f.

to non-legal historico-political factors, to what a plain lawyer might well call sheer chance. Because of its power and proximity, England with its vastly different legal system would in all probability have been the dominating influence on the development of Scots law. But the war in the early 14th century between the two countries and the continuing hostility thereafter kept England and its influence closed to the Scots who turned to Continental Europe.[32] The same chance operates elsewhere. Thus, many modern African states have fundamentally a Common law or Civil law system depending on whether they were once ruled by the British on the one hand, or the French or Spanish on the other.

Secondly, we see that Nationalism may play an important rôle in determining which system will be the source of borrowing. Scotland accepted Roman law because of her resentment against England. Before the War of Independence Scots law had looked to England, and did so again in recent times when tensions eased. There seems to be an element of national fervour when a modern Scot, lamenting the acceptance of rules of English law and trying to stem the tide, says 'But, alas, . . . we in Scotland have gone a-whoring after some very strange gods.'[33] Nationalism has also played a part in the recent increased importance attached to the old Roman-Dutch authorities in South Africa.

Thirdly, the reception shows the importance in this connection of the lack of a strong native law and the absence of system. It is a characteristic of jurists to rely upon precedent of one kind or another, and upon authority. English case law is the supreme and best-known example. Lower courts are bound by the decisions of higher courts, and until 1966 the House of Lords was bound by its own previous decision.[34] The Roman jurists habitually cited lists of others in support.[35] Cicero teases his friend, the jurist Trebatius, who in December 54 B.C. was with the army in Northern Gaul: 'I am much afraid you are shivering in your winter quarters; wherefore I think you should make use of a bright hearth – Mucius and Manilius are of the same opinion –

[32] And when the Parliaments of England and Scotland were united in 1707, the Scots insisted on keeping a separate legal system, as they still do.

[33] T. B. Smith, 'Strange Gods: The Crisis of Scots Law as a Civilian System', *Studies Critical and Comparative* (Edinburgh, 1962), p. 72.

[34] See Lord Chancellor's statement of 26th July 1966: Practice Statement (H.L.) (Judicial Precedent) [1966] 1 W.L.R. 1234; [1966] All ER 77.

[35] See the texts in the *Fragmenta Vaticana*. The *Digest* gives rather a false picture since the lists there have been abridged.

especially since you are not well supplied with cloaks.'[36] The Valentinian Law of Citations of A.D. 426[37] made authoritative all the writings of five much earlier jurists, Ulpian, Paul, Papinian, Modestinus and Gaius; in a period of reduced standards, authority was sought from earlier and better days. Likewise, outside Rome, in a country where legal development is poor, authority will be sought from other places and also from other times.

But it should not be overlooked that even a highly developed system may seek authority from another country. Highly revealing are the words of Tindal C.J. in the English case of *Acton* v. *Blundell*:[38] 'The Roman law forms no rule, binding in itself, upon the subjects of these realms; but, in deciding a case upon principle where no direct authority can be cited from our books, it affords no small evidence of the soundness of the conclusion at which we have arrived, if it proves to be supported by that law, the fruit of the researches of the most learned men, the collective wisdom of ages and the groundwork of the municipal law of most of the countries of Europe.

'The authority of one at least of the learned Roman lawyers appears decisive upon the point in favour of the defendants; of some others the opinion is expressed with more obscurity.'

Fourthly, a total mistake as to the meaning of the rules which it is thought are being borrowed need not stop the creation of a new doctrine nor prevent it becoming authoritative and important. A further instructive example can be drawn from South Africa, from malicious desertion as a ground of divorce. The fundamental case is *Walters* v. *Walters*.[39] Curlewis J.'s opinion stated: 'But in our law the desertion must be malicious, and it is not sufficient for one spouse merely to state that the other spouse has deserted him or her. It must be proved that the desertion, either from its inception or by reason of its continuance, is malicious, that is, that the deserter had no sufficient cause, so far as the complaining party was concerned, for the desertion. *Brouwer* (*de Jure Connubiorum*, 2. 18. 12) gives the following definition:[40] *Malitiosus desertor est, qui nulla justa aut necessaria causa coactus, ex animi quadam levitate et malitia, vel impatientia freni conjugalis, uxoris et liberorum*

---

[36] *ad fam.* 7. 10. Mucius and Manilius were well-known jurists.

[37] *C.Th.* I. 4. 3.   [38] (1843) M. & W. 324 at p. 353.

[39] [1911] T.P.D. 42.

[40] 'A *malitiosus desertor* is a person who, compelled by no just or necessary cause, from a certain levity of mind or wickedness or impatience of the conjugal yoke, casts aside the care of wife and children, deserts them and goes away without the intention of returning.'

curam abjicit, eos deserit, et oberrat sine animo redeundi. And it follows that, if the party who complains of having been deserted has given sufficient cause for the act of desertion, such desertion cannot be said to be malicious.' The South African court was clearly seeking to follow Brouwer[41] and the 17th-century Dutch law. But a more careful and fuller reading of the *de Jure Connubiorum* (first published at Amsterdam in 1665) would have shown that for Brouwer no desertion is ever justified and no deserter is ever compelled by a just or necessary cause – the right thing to do if one's spouse behaves badly is petition for a separation from bed and board. For Brouwer *malitiosus desertor* means a deliberate deserter: the misleading words of Brouwer's definition are due to borrowings in his turn from the rather earlier German, Carpzovius (1595–1666).[42] The older South African cases had, in fact, followed the Roman-Dutch rule,[43] though a rather different attitude, influenced by English judicial opinion, becomes apparent from about 1908.[44, 45]

Another instance would be the very concept of *furtum usus*, theft of use, which is discussed in many modern systems, especially those which derive from Roman law. Most modern systems, including France, Germany and Scotland now – whatever they once did – declare that (in general) *furtum usus* is not a crime,[46] though others such as Italy do make it criminal.[47] Which attitude is adopted does not matter here since

[41] 1625–1683.

[42] *Definitiones ecclesiasticae seu consistoriales* (first published at Leipzig in 1645), 2. 11. 192. 4.

[43] Cf., above all, *Mostert* v. *Mostert,* Searle Reports (Cape Supreme Court) II (1853–1856) 128; *Heathershaw* v. *Heathershaw,* Roscoe Reports (Cape Supreme Court) I (1861–1867) 186.   [44] Cf. *Nield* v. *Nield* [1908] T.S. 1113.

[45] For a fuller account of the whole development, see A. Watson, 'The Development of Marital Justifications for *Malitiosa Desertio* in Roman-Dutch Law', *L.Q.R.* lxxix (1963), pp. 87ff. A similar mistranslation and misunderstanding, this time of D. 36. 2. 26. 1 (Papinian 9 resp.), is responsible for the South African rule that it is possible for a fiduciary to be burdened with administrative duties without having any rights of enjoyment for himself: for this development see P. Frere-Smith, *Manual of South African Trust Law* (Durban, 1953), pp. 48ff.

[46] For France, see, e.g., E. Garçon, *Code pénal annoté,* ii, 2nd edit. (Paris, 1956), p. 620 (refers to art. 379 of the *Code pénal*); for Germany, A. Schonke–H. Schröder, *Strafgesetzbuch Kommentar,* 13th edit. (Munich and Berlin, 1967), p. 1092 (refers to § 242 of the *Strafgesetzbuch*): for Scotland, G. H. Gordon, *The Criminal Law of Scotland* (Edinburgh, 1967), pp. 485f (leading case is *Murray* v. *Robertson,* 1927 J.C.I.).

[47] *Codice penale,* art. 626; cf., e.g., F. Mantovani, in *Novissimo Digesto italiano,* vii (Turin, 1961), s.v. *Furto (Diritto penale comune),* p. 715.

we are concerned only with the concept as such. The name, of course, is Latin, and most jurists concerned with the modern law believe that *furtum usus* was a Roman concept and term which they now either accept or reject. This is just not the case. The expression *furtum usus* does not appear in the Roman sources, and the Romans had no such concept but only the basic idea of *furtum*, theft. Admittedly the Roman delict of *furtum* was committed even when the thief merely used the thing wrongfully and had no intention of depriving the owner permanently. But the offence was ordinary *furtum*, not such a thing as *furtum usus*, and hence damages would be the normal double (or quadruple) value of the thing, not a multiple of the owner's interest in the thing not being used or the thief's profit from the use.[48] The trichotomy – *furtum rei*, theft of a thing, *furtum usus*, theft of use, *furtum possessionis*, theft of possession – so dearly loved, especially in the 17th and 18th centuries, just did not exist in Roman law. Yet Voet could say, discussing Roman law, 'The definition of theft sufficiently shows that there can be theft not only of ownership, but also of use';[49] and A. Alison, of Scots law, 'We do not admit the *furtum usus* or *possessionis* of the Roman law.'[50] The source of this misconception is, as the quotation from Voet suggests, the Roman definition of *furtum*. Digest 47. 2. 1. 3 (Paul 39 *ad ed.*) reads: *Furtum est contrectatio rei fraudulosa lucri faciendi gratia vel ipsius rei vel etiam usus eius possessionisve &c*; 'Theft is the fraudulent handling of a thing with the intention of making a gain whether of the thing itself or even of its use or possession.' And the definition with the omission of *lucri faciendi gratia* is in Justinian's *Institutes*, 4. 1. 1. The trichotomy, of course, does not really appear in these definitions. The jurist responsible[51] for it is the famous French Huguenot, François Hotoman (1524–1590), whose commentary on the *Institutes* appeared in 1560, and who says on the relevant text, 'Theft is committed not only of the thing but also of use and possession.'[52] But this trichotomy of Hotoman would scarcely have become so pervasive had it not been for textual emendations of Haloander (died in 1531), whose editions of the *Digest* and *Institutes* both appeared

---

[48] See above all, Aulus Gellius, *Noctes Atticae*, 7. 15. 1, 2; cf. A. Watson, *The Law of Obligations in the Later Roman Republic* (Oxford, 1965), pp. 227f. See also, e.g., G. 3. 196; Valerius Maximus, 8. 2. 4.

[49] *Commentarius ad Pandectas*, 47. 2. 5: '*Nec tantum proprietatis, sed et usus furtum fieri, definitio satis ostendit.*'

[50] *Principles of the Criminal Law of Scotland* (Edinburgh, 1832), p. 271.

[51] But there are forerunners: e.g. Angelus de Ubaldis and Angelus Aretinus.

[52] '*Furtum non tantum rei, sed etiam usus ac possessionis committitur.*'

for the first time in 1529. With apparently no authority whatever in any manuscript he cut out the first *rei* in both works, and inserted *lucri faciendi gratia* in the *Institutes*. Since *contrectatio* requires to be followed by a genitive, *vel ipsius rei vel etiam usus eius possessionisve* had to be treated as being directly dependent upon that word: 'Theft is the fraudulent meddling[53] with a thing itself or even with its use or possession with a view to gain.' Although at first Haloander's emendations were not always accepted, his reading of the *Institutes* passage eventually prevailed and is to be found in almost all of the (extremely numerous) editions of the *Institutes* from the middle of the 16th to the 18th century.[54]

Fifthly, the enormous length of time during which Roman law has exercised its influence on Scotland shows that something can always be successfully borrowed – and adapted – from a highly developed system by a country even at a different stage of development. This remains true even if the parent system is not fully understood and even if the result is a barbarisation (and simplification). An equally good example can be found in the early Germanic codes enacted from the 5th century and which were also based on Roman law.[55]

Sixthly, a foreign rule can be successfully integrated into a very different system and even into a branch of the law which is constructed on very different principles from that of the donor. The clearest example in Scotland is the reception of rules of Roman property law grafted onto a very different local system. Again, a further illuminating instance can be drawn from South Africa. The trust, with its fragmentation of ownership, is one of the greatest English legal inventions and it had no real counterpart in European legal systems. It is, of course, extremely useful, particularly because of its flexibility, and it is much admired abroad.[56] Of the trust in South Africa, A. M. Honoré writes:[57] 'As a matter of history there is no doubt that trusts were introduced

---

[53] 'Handling', the proper translation here of *contrectatio*, became logically impossible.

[54] See for more detail of the process, A. Watson, 'The Definition of *furtum* and the Trichotomy', *T.v.R.* xxviii (1960), pp. 197ff.

[55] See the papers by E. Levy, 'Reflections on the First "Reception" of Roman Law in Germanic States', 'The Reception of Highly Developed Legal Systems by Peoples of Different Cultures', 'Vulgarization of Roman Law in the Early Middle Ages', now collected in *Gesammelte Schriften*, I (Cologne, 1963), pp. 201ff.

[56] Cf., e.g., C. De Wulf, *The Trust and Corresponding Institutions in the Civil Law* (Brussels, 1965), p. 27.

[57] *The South African Law of Trusts* (Cape Town, 1966), pp. 9ff.

into the Cape after the British occupation in 1815 and later spread to Natal and the rest of the country. The British officials and, later, the British settlers who came to the Cape in the early nineteenth century brought with them the words "trust" and "trustee" and the notion of a trust as it was then conceived in England and Scotland. . . . But though England and to a lesser extent Scotland is the historical source of the trust as a South African institution, it is another matter to assert that the rules of South Africa trust law are derived from English law. The truth is that there has been only a partial reception of English trust law. The most important conception which has been taken over is that of trusteeship as an office subject to public control. . . . The separation of the trustee's private property from the trust property is in some ways less complete in South African law than in English law but the principle of a dual capacity is recognised in both systems. Many of the subsidiary rules about the duties and liabilities of trustees have also been influenced by the English law on the subject, though there are differences. Other aspects of South African trust law are, however, quite un-English. In the first place the creation and revocation of trusts is governed by Roman-Dutch common law rules and some of the most characteristic features of the English law, such as the rule that a beneficiary need not accept in order for the trust to be irrevocable, have been consciously rejected.'

CHAPTER 8

MEANING AND AUTHORITY

In the previous chapter we saw that authority, respect for the donor system, played an important rôle in legal borrowing. At times this respect might lead to odd results.

In Holland the reception of Roman law was much more complete than was the case in Scotland. Speaking broadly, one can say that Roman law was applied unless the particular rule had been expressly repealed by statute or had fallen into desuetude. Moreover, the law there by the 17th century (and before) was much more a 'learned law', the scholars had much more authority and, indeed, had far greater understanding of Roman law. This makes particularly interesting those situations where either Roman law did not provide a precedent or the Dutch wished to observe a different rule. One instance will suffice. There is a surprising lack in the Roman legal sources of texts dealing with the effects of alcohol,[1] and none at all on the legal effects of making an agreement or entering upon marriage while drunk. Presumably, intoxication was regarded as irrelevant. This created a problem – happily not insoluble – for jurists like Voet (1647–1713) who took the view that drunkenness bars agreement in sale unless intention persists. He cites[2] three Roman texts as authority. (1) D. 48. 19. 11. 2 (Marcian 2 de publicis iudiciis) which said that an injury may be caused with premeditation, on the spur of the moment, or by chance, and instances for the second a drunken brawl. (2) J. 2. 11. 1, that, since a soldier's will can be made without the usual formalities being observed, care has to be taken to ensure that the dead soldier had spoken with the intention of making a will. (3) D. 50. 17. 48 (Paul 35 ad edictum) that what is done or said in a fit of temper is not finally settled unless the intention is shown by perseverance, 'and so a wife who returns in a short time is not regarded as having divorced

---

[1] Six texts are all we have on intoxication, conduct influenced by alcohol, habitual drunkenness or heavy drinking; A. Watson, 'Drunkenness in Roman Law', *Sein und Werden im Recht*, edited by W. G. Becker and L. Schnorr v. Carolsfeld (Berlin, 1970), pp. 381ff.

[2] *Commentarius ad Pandectas*, 18. 1. 4.

her husband'. Not one of these three texts refers to sale or any other contract, and only one concerns drunkenness.

Though Voet obviously feels that Roman authority is needed, the rule itself that drunkenness bars agreement in sale was no novelty in Holland. It already appears in its full form, without citation of authority, in Grotius, *Inleiding tot de Hollandsche Rechtsgeleertheyd*, 3. 14. 5.

A very different case, a blatant example of intellectual opportunism, can be found in an exploitation of absolute ignorance. The old Roman *lex Aquilia* had three chapters. Chapter one concerned the killing of slaves and herd animals, chapter three the wounding of such, and the injury and destruction of all other things animate and inanimate. Chapter two gave an action to the *stipulator* (the principal creditor in a contract of *stipulatio*) against the *adstipulator* (an alternative person to whom the debtor could make payment) who released the debtor from the *stipulatio* and did not hand over what had been promised to the *stipulator*.[3] Chapter two was obsolete in classical Roman law and all the information on it which existed for later generations (until the discovery of the Verona codex of Gaius' *Institutes* in 1816) were two texts which said that the chapter was not in use: D. 9. 2. 27. 4 (Ulpian *18 ad ed.*), *Huius legis secundum quidem capitulum in desuetudinem abiit*; J. 4. 3. 12, *Caput secundum legis Aquiliae in usu non est*. Inevitably there was much speculation as to the provisions of the chapter. A very careful academic jurist like Noodt (1647–1725) could say that he had never discovered what it was about though he knew the views of others, and that two vices were to be avoided; to consider the unknown as known, and to devote great labour to obscure and unnecessary matters.[4] But other, more practical, men would not only find the probable content but discover contemporary uses for it. The influential Voet is a good example. He suggests[5] it likely that chapter two dealt with the moral corruption of slaves; 'just as the first chapter was concerned with the extinction of the whole slave, the second with the more noble part of him, that is the corruption of his soul, the third with the less noble part, that is an injury to his body, a scheme not inharmonious'.[6] He goes on to point out that chapter two was never

---

[3] G. 3. 215; cf. above all, H. Lévy-Bruhl, 'Le Deuxième Chapitre de la loi Aquilia', *R.I.D.A.* v (1958), pp. 507ff.

[4] *Liber singularis ad legem Aquiliam*, cap. 13.

[5] *Ad pandectas*, 9. 2. 5.

[6] '*Sic ut primum quidem caput de toto servo perempto, secundum de parte ejus nobiliore, puta animo corrupto, tertium autem de parte minus nobili, corpore scilicet laeso, methodo quâdam non inconcinnâ conceptum fuerit.*'

abrogated but simply fell into disuse when a better remedy, the *actio servi corrupti*, was introduced. And he argues that on occasion the action under chapter two remained useful and indeed more useful than the *actio servi corrupti*. He concludes that even in his own day chapter two could have its uses if it was extended by analogy to the corruption of the morals of sons, monks, subjects, vassals and the like.[7]

One of the strangest episodes ever in the transplanting of laws is to be found in the 8th century A.D., in book I. 4 of the *Lex Romana Raetica Curiensis*[8] which was intended for the Roman people of eastern Switzerland, and was used in the Tyrol and northern Italy. The *Lex* was not a public statute but was written by a private individual who had no intention of innovating but wished to explain the old Roman laws as they were used in his day. The basis of his work was not the original Roman sources but the compilation ordered in A.D. 506 by King Alaric II, which is known as the *Lex Romana Visigothorum* (or the *Breviarium Alaricianum*). Book I. 4 of the *Lex Raetica* seeks to give the provisions of the famous Roman Law of Citations[9] of A.D. 426. This, in a period of diminished legal standards, had made authoritative all the writings of five great classical jurists, Ulpian, Paul, Papinian, Modestinus and Gaius – all of whom had lived at least two centuries before – and gave weight to the writings of jurists, such as Scaevola, who were cited by one of the five. When the five expressed conflicting opinions the view of the majority was to prevail, when those who had expressed an opinion were equally divided the view favoured by Papinian was to prevail, and when they were equally divided and Papinian had expressed no opinion the judge could follow the side he preferred. Now in the *Lex Raetica* Papinian appears – not for the first time – as Papian, Gaius as Gagius, and Scaevola as Scifola. Odder still, the Law of Citations is understood to mean that each party to a law suit ought to produce supporters, and the party who has the greatest number of good men is to win. If they have an equal number of

7 '*Neque haec de capitis secundi sententiâ disseruisse piget, cum illa ita explanatum suâ etiam nunc non careat utilitate, si exemplo actionis de servo corrupto, quin et ejus, quae ex primo ac tertio hujus legis capite data est, ad corruptos filiorum familias, monachorum, subjectorum, vasallorum, similiumque mores cum Jurisconsultis et Interpretibus porrigatur.*'

8 The *Lex* is edited by K. Zeumer in *Monumenta Germaniae Historica, Legum V* (Hanover, 1875–1889), pp. 289ff. I. 4 of the *Lex* is quoted by P. Vinogradoff, *Roman Law in Mediaeval Europe*, 2nd edit. (Oxford, 1929), pp. 146f; and discussed, pp. 21ff.

9 *C.Th.* I. 4. 3.

supporters, that party is to win whose claim is backed by an opinion of Papian. As Vinogradoff says,[10] 'it is clear that the paragraph as it stands neither corresponds to the original nor could be put into practice'. What we have, though, is a primitive Germanic form of compurgation explained very oddly in Roman law terms and made to rest on Roman law authority.

[10] *Roman Law*, p. 23.

CHAPTER 9

LO CODI

In the early Middle Ages, in the centuries immediately succeeding
the rediscovery of Justinian's *Corpus Iuris Civilis*,[1] the published commentaries on the *Digest* and many of those on the *Code* were published
lectures.[2] The mediaeval jurists did write books as such,[3] but these
were almost always manuals on procedure which might be expanded
to take in some substantive law: the *Speculum* of Durantis is a good
example. The one exception to all this is the *Summa Codicis* which is
always a book written for publication and is not a lecture-course. Of
Summae Codicis we can mention the *Summa Perusina* which seems to
date basically from the 8th century though later notes and glosses
are incorporated into the text; more especially, from the period of the
glossators, the *Summa Codicis Trecensis*, perhaps of the middle of the
12th century, the *Summae* of Rogerius, of Placentinus and of Bassianus,
all of the later 12th century, and above all of Azo in the early 13th
century; it also seems proper to consider Vacarius' *liber pauperum* of
the mid-12th century as a *Summa Codicis*.[4] The *Summae* are concerned
only with the first nine books[5] of Justinian's *Code* perhaps because the
last three were not known as early as the others, perhaps because of
academic tradition since the professors giving the *ordinaria* lectured
only on the first nine books, perhaps because the last three books are
concerned with administrative law.

The word *Summa* is itself a very vague one and does not indicate
any particular form, and the term *Summa Codicis* was originally
Summae Codicis. It was a collection of *summae* and in this sense the
summa began life as a long gloss attached to a title in the *Corpus Juris*,
and which assembled for the benefit of the reader the textual material
scattered in the rest of the *Corpus Juris*, relevant to the subject matter

[1] Though the term is much later.
[2] Indeed, it is difficult to estimate the part played in their publication by the
jurists whose names are associated with the commentaries.
[3] Here we are ignoring glosses which are among their outstanding productions.
[4] Mr. J. L. Barton tells me that, despite De Zulueta, he very much doubts
whether the *liber Pauperum* was used as a lecture course.
[5] The *Summa Perusina* only with the first eight.

of the title. The *Summa Codicis* brought these *summae* together and it might be considered as a companion to the *Code*.[6] Hence as in Azo's *Summa Codicis* there may be as many references to the Digest as to the *Code*. The reader is assumed to have the text of the *Code* in front of him, and to need not the information which is in the *Code* but the information which is not in it. A rather interesting conclusion[7] seems to follow. The full *Corpus Juris* is lectured upon,[8] but if the student is proposing to improve his knowledge by reading, then the assumption seems to be that the obvious course for him is to go through the *Code*, and that the sort of book most useful to him is one which enables him to go through the *Code* with the most profit to himself.

One of the most important of these *Summae Codicis* was first mentioned in print in 1838,[9] and the attention of mediaevalists was first directed to it in 1891. This is *lo Codi* which was written in Provençal probably around 1149.[10] Much remains obscure about this work which has not yet been published in its original language, but it is clearly close to the *Summa Trecensis* and the *Summa Codicis* of Rogerius,[11] and it was probably written at Arles.[12] What is remarkable about *lo Codi* is its influence – not on contemporary practice in Provence where it is not evidenced[13] – but later and elsewhere. It was translated into French, Dauphinois, Latin, Catalan and Castilian,[14] and one

[6] Cf. H. Kantorowicz, *Studies in the Glossators of the Roman Law* (Cambridge, 1938), pp. 146f.

[7] For which I am indebted to Mr. J. L. Barton.

[8] Though some parts are dealt with in more detail than others.

[9] C. Giraud, *Recherches sur le droit de propriété chez les Romains sous la République et sous l'Empire* (Aix, 1838), pp. 142ff.

[10] The evidence on which arguments for dating rests is the clause, '*Peire, sias mos herez soz tal condicion, se Fraga sera presa entro ad un an o entro a dos.*' ('Pierre, you will be my heir on condition that Fraga is taken in one year or two years.') Fraga is a small town in Spain near Lérida and was a bastion of the Saracens, until it was taken in 1149 by Raymond-Béranger IV of Barcelona who also controlled Provence. For the arguments on the date see R. Feenstra, 'A propos d'un nouveau manuscrit de la version latine du Code (Ms Lucques, Bibl. Feliniana 437)', *Studi Gratiana*, xiii (1967), *Collectanea Stephan Kuttner*, iii, pp. 57ff at pp. 65ff.

[11] Cf. Feenstra, 'Nouveau Manuscrit', p. 63. That article contains a full bibliography of previous researches on *lo Codi*, and discusses the major points of interest.

[12] Cf. Feenstra, 'Nouveau Manuscrit', pp. 67ff.

[13] Cf. the works cited by Feenstra, 'Nouveau Manuscrit', p. 63.

[14] For the manuscripts of these translations see J. Prawer, 'Étude préliminaire sur les sources et la composition du "livre des Assises des bourgeois"', *R.H.D.* xxxii (1954), pp. 198ff and again pp. 358ff at p. 205, n. 5; to these should be added the Latin translation discovered by Feenstra, 'Nouveau Manuscrit'.

modern scholar has raised the question whether any legal work, with the exception of that of Gratian, has been so widely diffused.[15] The sole Latin manuscript found in Italy seems never to have left Tuscany.[16] On a practical level its influence is plain on the Charter of Arles, on the Coutumes of Tortosa (in Catalonia), on the Fors[17] of Béarn and of Morlaas, and there are even late extracts and translations in the 15th century in the Coutumes of Anjou and of the Marne, and in the strange *Lois de l'Empereur* which come from the Béarn. A Latin text related to *lo Codi* is preserved in Venetian legislation.[18] Most striking of all is the influence on the *Livre des Assises des Bourgeois* which is the work of a jurist writing at Acre in the middle of the 13th century; 63 of the 237 chapters are a direct translation of *lo Codi*, and in a further 59 there is some dependence.[19]

The foregoing shows the extreme importance of Justinian's *Code* for legal development in the early Middle Ages, and the influence of *lo Codi* itself throws two facts into sharp relief. First of all, the legal rules of a work like Justinian's *Code* might be widely disseminated through an intermediary source which is less complex and more on a level with contemporary needs. Secondly, since *lo Codi* was not an official compilation or legislation, it appears that the source for a transplant need not itself have been anywhere of binding force.

The *Digest* was, of course, also far from unimportant in the early Middle Ages. It is enough to remember the achievement of the *glossa magna* of Accursius. Moreover, throughout the Universities of Europe the *libri ordinarii* were the *Digestum Vetus*[20] and the *Code*, and the former was at least as important as the latter.[21] Yet the existence and nature of the *Summae Codicis* and the absence of any *Summa Digesti* suggest that attention was directed rather towards the *Code*. There is a contrast here with later periods, with the Humanists of the 16th

---

[15] Prawer, 'Étude préliminaire', p. 205.

[16] Cf. Feenstra, 'Nouveau Manuscrit', p. 77, n. 79, and p. 81.

[17] i.e. Customs.

[18] For all this see Prawer, 'Étude préliminaire', pp. 205f and the references in p. 205, n. 5.

[19] Cf. Prawer, 'Étude préliminaire', especially at pp. 205ff and 363ff; 'Étude sur le droit des *Assises de Jérusalem*: Droit de confiscation et droit d'exhérédation', *R.H.D.* xxxix (1961), pp. 520ff at pp. 534ff. The last-named study has a valuable confrontation of texts from pp. 536ff.

[20] That is, books I to XXIV. 2 of the *Digest*.

[21] It may be a pointer that in mediaeval Cambridge the fee for a course on the *Digestum Vetus* was somewhat larger.

century and with the great Dutch jurists of the 17th century, who in their turn appear to stress Justinian's *Digest*. The explanation of this difference is probably not hard to find. The *Digest* consists of juristic writings almost exclusively from the so-called classical period, from Augustus to about A.D. 235, the *Code*, on the other hand, of Imperial rulings basically from the post-classical period, from around 235 to Justinian. Apart from emphasis and style[22] there are two main differences between these works. Almost half of the texts in the *Code* date from a time after the Emperors[23] had become Christian whereas those in the *Digest* are earlier, hence Christianity appears prominently in the *Code* but not in the *Digest*. The *Code*, but not the *Digest*, can be regarded as a Christian law book. Again in the classical period – to speak very generally – one can say that differences in social standing among free men were not reflected in differences in legal status. But in the post-classical period, after Diocletian and more particularly with Constantine, individuals came to be fixed in rigid, static and largely hereditary groups each with their own particular rights and duties, whether they were *coloni* (rather like serfs) or shipowners or members of a town council, and so on. This strict stratification of people is not much apparent in the *Digest*, but is in the *Code*. Both in its Christianity and in its representation of social groups, the *Code* was more akin to the spirit of the early Middle Ages than was the *Digest*. Later other social factors, such as the weakening of the legal privilege of specified groups, caused the *Digest* to predominate.

The lesson for us in this is that when a large, complex collection such as the *Corpus Juris Civilis* is used as a legal quarry by many generations, each age may be attracted by something different and will concentrate much of its efforts on what seems important fot it. An important source for borrowing from is not to be regarded as monolithic.

[22] The *Digest* texts are much more urbane.
[23] 2,019 as against 2,664: but the bulk of the former is greater.

THE EARLY LAW OF THE MASSACHUSETTS BAY COLONY[1]

The fishing and farming venture established at Cape Ann in 1623 was a failure, but some of the members of the company which had set it up were unwilling to abandon entirely the idea of a settlement, and they sent over more colonists. Difficulties arose as to the legal basis of the settlement and the rights of the members, and the colonists asked for a charter. This, thanks to the influence of the Earl of Warwick, was granted by King Charles I on 14th March 1629. *Inter alia* the charter provided:[2] 'AND wee doe, of our further grace, certen knowledg and meere motion, give and graunt to the saide Governor and Company, and their successors, That it shall and maie be lawfull to and for the Governor or Deputie Governor and such of the Assistantes and Freemen of the said Company for the time being as shalbe assembled in any of their Generall Courtes aforesaide, or in any other Courtes to be specially summoned and assembled for that purpose, or the greater parte of them (whereof the Governor or Deputie Governor and six of the Assistantes, to be alwaies seaven,) from tyme to tyme to make, ordeine, and establishe all manner of wholesome and reasonable orders, lawes, statutes, and ordinances, directions, and instructions not contrarie to the lawes of this our realme of England . . .'

The colonists must not be thought of as ignorant, uneducated men. It has been estimated that about one-tenth of those who came with Winthrop in 1630 were above yeomen in social rank, nearly one-fifth were apprentices and indentured servants, and the rest were small farmers, and labourers.[3] Many of the leading settlers had considerable business experience and several had legal training. John Winthrop, the leader, had himself been a justice of the peace, was admitted to

---

[1] See, in general, G. L. Haskins, *Law and Authority in Early Massachusetts* (New York, 1960); and the articles by various authors in *Essays in the History of Early American Law*, edited by D. H. Flaherty (Chapel Hill, N.C. 1969).

[2] The charter is conveniently reproduced in E. S. Morgan (ed.), *The Founding of Massachusetts* (Indianapolis, 1964), pp. 303ff. The passage quoted here is to be found on p. 319.

[3] Haskins, *Law and Authority*, p. 98.

Gray's Inn, and was an attorney in the Court of Wards and Liveries which gave him experience of legal drafting. Richard Bellingham had been Recorder of Boston in Lincolnshire, John Winthrop, Jr., was a barrister of the Inner Temple, William Pynchon had been a justice of the peace, John Humfry was a member of Lincoln's Inn and is said to have been an attorney in the Court of Wards and Liveries, and Nathaniel Ward is reputed to have been an utter barrister.[4]

The separatist tendencies of the colonists led them away from the Charter provision which has been quoted, and from the beginning they showed considerable independence of spirit. They stopped appeals from the courts to England, and passed a number of laws on account of the particular conditions prevailing in the colony: shortage of labour and goods led to regulation of wages and prices; scarcity of coined money resulted in corn and beaver being made legal tender, and in obligations under 12 pence bullets were to pass as farthings; inheritance of land was divisible and not subject to primogeniture. Particular events can also be shown to have affected the law.[5] In all these matters, a supporter of the 'Volksgeist' theory of law would find much comfort, even though, inevitably, the most fruitful source of law was English law.

After various vicissitudes a code of law was issued in 1648 under the title, *The General Lawes and Liberties Concerning the Inhabitants of the Massachusets*.[6] This, the earliest code of the modern Western legal world, deserves to be much better known.[7] It was drafted by three county committees with a total of 18 members. Of these at least John Winthrop, Richard Bellingham and Nathaniel Ward had legal training, and Ward, John Cotton, John Norton and Thomas Shepard, were the colony's most prominent ministers. The Bible was one source of inspiration.

The Bible as a direct source of law can be most clearly seen – indeed is only readily apparent – on the paragraph on 'Capital Lawes'. 14 of the 15 sections are expressly based on scripture both as to substance and penalty, the fifteenth – on rape of a maid or single woman – deriv-

---

[4] Haskins, *Law and Authority*, pp. 105f.

[5] Haskins, *Law and Authority*, pp. 115ff.

[6] The most convenient edition is *The Laws and Liberties of Massachusetts*, introduction by M. Farrand (Cambridge, Mass., 1929) which reprints the 1648 edition.

[7] In many ways it is very different from the later European codes. One curious feature is that the arrangement of topics is alphabetical, an order which is taken from English abridgements.

ing from a rule of 1641.[8] Death is therefore laid down as the penalty for Idolatrie, Witch-craft, Blasphemie, Murther, Poysoning, Bestial-itie, Sodomie, Adulterie with a married or espoused wife, Man-stealing, False-wittnes, Conspiracie, Child curse or smite parents, and a Rebellious Son.[9] Some of the provisions betray interesting diver-gences from their models.

> 8. If any man LYETH WITH MAN-KINDE as he lieth with a woman, both of them have committed abomination, they both shall surely be put to death: unles the one partie were forced (or be under fourteen years of age in which case he shall be seveerly punished) Levit. 20. 13.

> Leviticus, 20. 13.[10] If a man also lie with mankind, as he lieth with a woman, both of them have committed an abomination: they shall surely be put to death; their blood shall be upon them.

Thus the Massachusetts code exempts from the death penalty males who were forced or under the age of fourteen, while no such quali-fications are expressed in Leviticus. There is no point in searching for a precise historical precedent for the first qualification. But for the second we might look to English law of which Sir Edward Coke (1552–1634) says: 'If the party buggered be within the age of discretion, it is no felony in him, but in the agent only.'[11] And the age of discretion was then fourteen. None the less, the Massachusetts' provision seems to differ in two important respects from the English Law. First, in the colony the person under fourteen was still regarded as guilty of an offence (and was to be severely punished) whereas in England he was not. Secondly, Coke makes it plain that it is only the passive party under fourteen who does not commit the felony[12] whereas the colony's

[8] But Deuteronomy 22. 25 does lay down the death penalty for the rape of a betrothed girl.

[9] A broadside, *The Capitall Lawes of New-England* printed in London in 1643 and claiming to have been first printed in New England – no copies from New England survive – gives the law 'in force' in 1641, 1642. Death is there also expressly laid down as the penalty for 'carnall copulation with any woman-childe under ten yeares old' (§10) and for the rape of 'any maid or woman that is law-fully married or contracted' (§11; Deut. 22. 25 etc.), but not for a child who curses or smites his parents or for a rebellious son. Only two copies of this broad-side are known, in the British Museum and the Harvard Law School Library, but it is reprinted in *Harvard Law School Bulletin* (February 1956), p. 11.

[10] Authorised Version, which is the translation apparently used for the code.

[11] *The Third Part of the Institutes of the Laws of England* (first published London, 1644), chap. 10.

[12] The irrebuttable presumption, so important in rape, that a male is incapable of erection until fourteen is later.

provision seems from its language – though it is not free from ambiguity – to exclude both active and passive participants from the death penalty. In §8 'unles the one partie were forced' obviously exempts only the passive party, while 'or be under fourteen etc.' is separated from this by brackets.

§14. If a man have a stubborn or REBELLIOUS SON, of sufficient years and understanding (*viz*) sixteen years of age, which will not obey the voice of his Father, or the voice of his Mother, and that when they have chastened him will not harken unto them: then shal his Father & Mother being his natural parents, lay hold on him, & bring him to the Magistrates assembled in Court & testifie unto them, that their Son is stubborn and rebellious & will not obey their voice and chastisement, but lives in sundry notorious crimes, such a son shal be put to death. Deut. 21. 20. 21.

Deuteronomy 21. 18. If a man have a stubborn and rebellious son, which will not obey the voice of his father, or the voice of his mother, and that when they have chastened him, will not hearken unto them:

19. Then shall his father and his mother lay hold on him, and bring him out unto the elders of his city, and unto the gate of his place;

20. And they shall say unto the elders of his city, This our son is stubborn and rebellious, he will not obey our voice; he is a glutton and a drunkard.

21. And all the men of his city shall stone him with stones, that he die. . . .

Again, the Puritan variations – even in the (unexpressed) method of execution – are obvious. This time the provision of the code had no parallel in contemporary English law. Nor, although some of the compilers of the code were well-versed in Hebrew,[13] are the variations to be found in post-biblical Jewish sources. Certainly the verses of Deuteronomy were subject to rabbinical interpretation, but the variations were different. Thus, the *Mishnah, Sanhedrin*, 8.1 has: ' "A stubborn and rebellious son" – when can he be condemned as a stubborn and rebellious son? From the time that he can produce two hairs until he grows a beard (the lower one and not the upper one [is meant]; howbeit the Sages spoke in modest language), for it is written, *If a man have a son*; – a son and not a daughter, a son and not a man; a minor[14] is exempt since he has not yet come within the scope of the commandments.'[15]

Similar deviations from the Old Testament provisions are to be

[13] At least Ward and Cotton; cf. Haskins, *Law and Authority*, p. 143.
[14] Later this was interpreted to mean a boy under thirteen years and a day.
[15] H. Danby's translation; *The Mishnah* (Oxford, 1933), p. 394.

found in some of the other sections. Thus, for idolatry the penalty is death only if 'after legal conviction' a man worship another God (§1);[16] for children who curse or smite their parents the offence is capital 'unles it can be sufficiently testified that the Parents have been very unchristianly negligent in the education of such children; or so provoked them by extream, and cruel correction; that they have been forced therunto to preserve themselves from death or maiming.' (§14).[17]

The significance of all this is that these Puritan settlers sought to follow the word of God as closely as they reasonably could, yet in their code of laws there is only one paragraph, that on capital punishment which is closely modelled on the Bible. Even in that, they find it necessary to insert a further capital offence, and to accept important variations on several of the biblical provisions. Moreover, the Bible contains capital offences which are not so punished under the code: incest,[18] sabbath-breaking,[19] insubordination to supreme authority.[20, 21]

English law exercised its influence through the Common Law, through English local customs, and through the Court of Chancery and other courts.[22]

The English common law of the time was partly statutory but mainly case law which was enshrined in reports which in turn became the basis for abridgements and treatises. The colonists had considerable knowledge of English statute: thus the Statute of Artificers (1563) and the Poor Law (1601) were the basis of the colony's system of apprenticeship, the Statute of Labourers (1563) influenced the colony's law of employment; and the importance of the Statute of Uses (1535) can be seen in Massachusetts' conveyances. Moreover, Joseph Hills claimed that when he was revising the draft code of 1648 he perused all the statute laws of England as they were collected in F. Pulton[23] and took all he conceived were suitable for the commonwealth.[24] We do not

---

[16] The code refers to Exodus 22. 20; Deuteronomy 13. 6, 10; 17. 2, 6.

[17] The code refers to Exodus 21. 17; Leviticus 20. 9; Exodus 21. 15.

[18] Leviticus, 20. 11, 12.

[19] Exodus 31. 15; 35.2; Numbers, 15. 32–36.

[20] Deuteronomy 17. 12.

[21] Earlier, a code drafted by John Cotton but never promulgated did propose the death penalty for these and also for perjury and treason.

[22] For all that follows see Haskins, *Law and Authority*, pp. 163ff.

[23] *A Collection of sundrie Statutes, frequent in use*, first published in London in 1618.

[24] Cf. Haskins, *Law and Authority*, pp. 133f.

know in detail which English textbooks the colonists had, but the General Court had ordered two copies of *Coke on Littleton*, *Coke on Magna Carta*, *Coke's Reports*, *New Terms of the Law*, *Book of Entries* and Dalton's *Country Justice*.

The colony's commercial law was very much based on English common law and the Law Merchant, for instance bills of lading and bills of exchange. English local custom was important especially as regards inheritance and recording of deeds. The system in Massachusetts seems to be derived from a conglomeration of customs from various districts of England, and not from one place. The Courts of Chancery, Star Chamber and others were at their most influential with regard to procedure.

The *Laws and Liberties* are full of English technical legal terms and concepts: barratrie, distresse, escheats, replevin, trespasse, chattels real and personal and so on. In an earlier chapter of this book the influence of the arrangement of Justinian's *Institutes* on the systematics of Scots law and other systems was stressed. Likewise the arrangement of the *Laws and Liberties* betrays its origins. It is ordered – strangely, we might think, for a code – alphabetically, beginning: Abilitie, Actions, Age, Ana-Baptists, Appeale, Appearance, Non-Appearance, Arrests, Attachments, Bakers, etc. This arrangement is that which had recently been adopted in a number of English abridgements, from the fifteenth century onwards.[25] The system has obvious faults, but Holdsworth[26] has stressed its advantages, one of which may have had particular relevance for the colonists: the alphabetical arrangement makes it easy to find the required provision, whereas in what might be regarded as a logical systematic code a person not trained in the logic of the system has great difficulty in tracing the relevant rule.[27]

[25] It is still found in Halsbury's *Laws of England*.

[26] 'Charles Viner and the Abridgments of English Law', *LQR*, xxxix (1923), pp. 17ff at pp. 37ff.

[27] Holdsworth says of the abridgers: 'They have used the alphabet to make English law accessible.'

CHAPTER II

ENGLISH LAW IN NEW ZEALAND[1]

The two islands forming New Zealand – especially North Island – were inhabited by the Maoris before their discovery by Europeans. Colonisation was very slow to start, but during the 1830s the number of Europeans, mainly missionaries, ex-convicts from Australia and whalers, living there without any organised system of law grew until it was around 2,000 at the beginning of 1840. In that year British sovereignty was proclaimed, and consequently New Zealand became subject to the laws of England in so far as they were reasonably applicable to the circumstances of the Dependency. And in 1858 the New Zealand Parliament provided in the English Laws Act that the laws of England, so far as they were applicable to the circumstances of the Colony, should be deemed to have been in force in the Colony since 14th January 1840. (The purpose of the Act was to remove doubts regarding the status in the Colony of the laws of New South Wales.) The law in New Zealand has been mainly directed towards the settlers from Britain, though usually it has also affected the Maoris. Here I want to outline the subsequent divergences of New Zealand law from English law, stopping – for reasons which I hope will become apparent – around 1950.

The law of marriage remained very similar to that of England. A change made in one jurisdiction was usually followed by a change in the other. The most significant alterations were in the prohibited degrees of marriage: New Zealand allowed marriage with a deceased wife's sister in 1880,[2] England in 1907;[3] with a deceased husband's brother in 1900,[4] England in 1921.[5] Decrees of divorce could be granted by the Supreme Court of New Zealand after the passing of the Divorce and Matrimonial Causes Act, 1867, which was based on,

[1] See, in general, J. L. Robson (and others), *New Zealand, The Development of its Laws and Constitution* (London, 1954); J. A. B. O'Keefe and W. L. Farrands, *Introduction to New Zealand Law* (Wellington, 1969).

[2] Deceased Wife's Sister Marriage Act.

[3] Deceased Wife's Sister's Marriage Act.

[4] Deceased Husband's Brother Marriage Act.

[5] Deceased Brother's Widow Marriage Act.

and very similar to, the English Matrimonial Causes Act of 1857. Unreasonably, the English common law of marriage, including the forms of celebration, was held to apply to Maoris.[6]

New Zealand was the first part of the British Commonwealth to pass a statute permitting adoption. The basic legislation, inspired by a law of Massachusetts, was the Adoption of Children Act of 1881, whereas England's Adoption of Children Act dates only from 1926. Under the influence of Scots law which itself derives from Roman law on this point,[7] legitimation by subsequent marriage was permitted by the Legitimation Act of 1894 provided there was no impediment to the marriage at the time of the birth. This qualification was removed by the Legitimation Act, 1921–22.[8] Legitimation by subsequent marriage became part of the law of England only by the Legitimacy Act 1926, and under that only if neither of the parents was married to a third party at the time of the birth. The restriction was removed by the Legitimacy Act, 1959.

A much more radical change in family law was brought about by the Testator's Family Maintenance Act 1900 (which was later re-enacted as Part II of the Family Protection Act, 1908). This gave the Supreme Court power to make orders which took precedence over the terms of a person's will to provide for the testator's wife, husband or children when he had not made proper provision for them. The Act has been interpreted widely, and the Supreme Court's power to make orders is not restricted to situations where members of the family are left destitute.[9] The Act has been followed in many Commonwealth countries,[10] in England by the Inheritance (Family Provision) Act 1938 which enabled the court to vary the terms of a will[11] if a dependant within a restricted class is not reasonably provided for. New Zealand's Family Homes Protection Act 1895 (Part I of the Family Protection

[6] *Rira Peti* v. *Ngaraihi Te Paku*, (1888) 7 N.Z.L.R. 235. And now Maori Purposes Act, 1951, section 8.

[7] The original provision dates from Constantine: C. 5. 27. 5. But there were other subsequent developments primarily by Justinian: C. 5. 27. 8, 10, 11: *Nov.* 12. 4; 8. 11; 78. 4.

[8] Now see Legitimation Act, 1939. The qualification was removed in Scotland by the Legitimation (Scotland) Act 1968.

[9] E.g. *Allardice* v. *Allardice* [1911] A.C. 730; *Allen* v. *Manchester* [1922] N.Z.L.R. 218. The present statute is the Family Protection Act 1955.

[10] See, e.g., B. Rudden, in *Annual Survey of Commonwealth Law 1967* (London, 1968), pp. 430ff. In most of Europe and in Scotland it has long been the case that dependants have been entitled to a proportion of the deceased's estate.

[11] Extended to cases of intestacy by the Intestates' Estates Act 1952.

Act 1908) permitted the owner of a dwelling-house to settle it as a family home exempt from creditors' claims so long as he was alive or any of his children was under 21. The provisions were supplemented and improved in 1950. No similar rule has been enacted in England.

Changes in contract law closely parallel those in England. But it is noticeable that New Zealand took the lead in restricting the powers of mortgagees on the outbreak of the First World War. Their Mortgages Extension Act was passed on 14th August 1914, while the United Kingdom's Increase of Rent and Mortgage Interest (War Restrictions) Act dates only from 23rd December 1915.

The law of torts has also remained very similar to the law of England. By legislation of 1880, however, re-enacted in the Dogs Restriction Act of 1908, the *scienter* rule was abolished for injuries caused by dogs. Changes in the English law of defamation led to very similar changes in New Zealand, and the New Zealand Contributory Negligence Act of 1947 is modelled on the English Act of 1945.

The greatest changes in private law took place in the area of property. In the 19th century – and even today – the law of real property and the law of conveyancing were the most traditional and complicated parts of English law. By contrast, New Zealand early simplified her real property law and introduced registration of conveyances of land long before England.

A simple method of conveyancing, applying throughout the colony, was introduced by an ordinance of the Legislative Council in 1842. The same ordinance also made important changes in the substantive law. This ordinance, it should be noted, accepted many of the suggestions of the 1829 report of the English commissioners on the law of real property. Since then there have been various modifications. The Land Registry Act 1860 introduced the Torrens system of registration of title but was rescinded in 1870 when a new and much improved Act was passed based on the original legislation of South Australia. In England the Land Registry Act 1862 introduced voluntary registration of title but in 1897 it was put on a more compulsory basis in areas for which an Order in Council is issued. The revised system is in the Land Registration Acts 1925 to 1971.[12]

The reception of English law in New Zealand is another instance of an immigrant population taking its law with it to an area where there was no comparable civilization. It should be remembered that

[12] Cf. *Cheshire's Modern Law of Real Property*, 11th edit., by E. H. Burn (London, 1972), pp. 102f.

New Zealand has always been the most English of the British countries overseas, and is the most homogeneous while England herself has been remarkably homogeneous until very recent years.

The most striking feature of New Zealand law to an outsider is how similar it has remained to English. Statutory changes in one are often (or even usually) mirrored in the other, even if only after a lapse of time. It is on account of this time lag that the present brief, very superficial, survey has stopped around 1950; an attempt to discuss recent developments would falsify the historical picture. The most obvious and lasting difference – simple land conveyancing in New Zealand – was largely due to the acceptance of proposals made by the English commissioners who were not so successful at home. The borrowings this time are mutual, and England has taken much from New Zealand. A more recent instance would be the 'Ombudsman' legislation; and the Divorce Reform Act, 1969 owes a great deal to the example of New Zealand's Matrimonial Proceedings Act 1963, and earlier legislation.[13]

But a particular New Zealand tendency is apparent. The legislature has been more prepared to humanise personal relationships by means of private law, than has its English counterpart.[14]

[13] See A. C. Holden, 'Divorce in the Commonwealth. A Comparative Study', *I.C.L.Q.* xx (1971), pp. 58ff.

[14] New Zealand has always been a leader in social legislation; cf. O'Keefe and Farrands, *Introduction*, pp. 191ff; M. D. Chrisp, 'Recent Developments in Family Law in New Zealand' in *Law and the Commonwealth*, edited by L. M. Singhvi, S. N. Jain and R. K. P. Shankardass (Delhi, 1971), pp. 540ff.

It might also be appropriate to mention that as a result of the Privy Council decision in *Farrell* v. *Bowman* (1887) 12 A.C. 643 plus subsequent legislation the Crown became liable in tort in New Zealand (and Australia): cf. P. W. Hogg, *Liability of the Crown* (Melbourne, 1971), pp. 6f.

CHAPTER 12

ROMAN LAW IN THE LATE REPUBLIC[1]

We have now, I think, looked at a sufficient number of general transplants and I should like to turn to an extreme instance of a non-transplant.

The great period of Roman legal development was the last two centuries of the Republic, especially the 1st century B.C. During this period, Roman law assumed the characteristics which have made it dominate all later Western law. The major innovations were the work of the higher magistrates, above all the Praetors, who issued annual Edicts, that is declarations of what they would or would not enforce in their courts.[2] The jurists also played a highly constructive role in interpreting very widely or narrowly according to their views of the needs of the case.[3] Statute was relatively unimportant.

It so happens that these same two centuries were the greatest period of Greek influence on Roman life. Rome's military conquest of Greece started in 200 B.C., and Roman literature began, it is said, with Livius Andronicus' [284 (?)–204(?) B.C.] translation of Homer's *Odyssey* while the outstanding works of the following generations, the comedies of Plautus [255(?)–184 B.C.] and Terence [190(?)–159(?) B.C.], are adaptations of Greek originals. The poetry at the end of the Republic also has obvious Greek forebears. Roman rhetoric comes almost entirely from Greek, though with its own emphasis, and philosophy, exemplified by Lucretius and Cicero, has little originality in substance. Greek models also predominate in the visual arts and in aesthetic appreciation. It is considered that most educated Romans were bilingual by the later 2nd century B.C.[4]

Most modern scholars would consider that Greek influence on Roman law was also considerable and these two centuries have even

---

[1] What follows is mainly a shortened and modified version of A. Watson, *Law Making in the Later Roman Republic* (Oxford, 1974), pp. 186ff.

[2] Cf., e.g., A. Watson, 'The Development of the Praetor's Edict', *Journal of Roman Studies*, lx (1970), pp. 105ff.

[3] Cf., e.g., A. Watson, 'Limits of Juristic Decision in the Later Roman Republic', in *Aufstieg und Niedergang der römischen Welt* I. ii, edit. by H. Temporini (Berlin, New York, 1972), pp. 215ff; 'Narrow, Rigid and Literal Interpretation in the Later Roman Republic', *T.v.R.* xxxvii (1969), pp. 351ff.

[4] Cf. H. H. Scullard, *From the Gracchi to Nero*, 3rd edit. (London, 1970), p. 10.

been designated 'The Hellenistic Period of Roman Jurisprudence'.[5] But when we attempt to pinpoint the results of this influence the results are disappointingly meagre.

Instances where it can be argued that Greek law has provided a model whether for a principle or a detail are very hard to find. One suggestion made was that the praetorian *actiones iniuriarum* (as opposed to the old civil law remedies established by the XII Tables) owe something to the Attic δίκη αἰκίας. When difficulties facing this view were pointed out, the idea of Greek influence did not disappear; instead the theory was propounded that the Alexandrian ὕβρις was the point of contact. But the divergences between the law of this city and Rome are just as great, and it is not even certain that the Alexandrian provisions antedate the Roman. It is very doubtful whether Greek influence on Roman *iniuria* will ever be convincingly demonstrated.[6]

The only other instance where it might be argued that Greek law influenced Roman law in the later Republic derives from the giving of earnest money (*arra*) in sale in the plays of Plautus. But for the suggestion to have validity it would have to be accepted (1) that the earnest money in the plays had a legal and not just a social function, (2) that consensual contracts had not yet been invented and it was the handing over of earnest money which brought the contract into existence and (3) that Plautus is presenting Roman rather than Attic law. Even if these three propositions could be accepted – and I *inter alios* would not accept them[7] – the influence of Greek law here would have been only transitory and would have lasted only until the introduction of the consensual contract of sale.[8]

At the very highest estimate then, the influence of Greek law on Roman law in the late Republic is very small. Similarly, the evidence for the influence of Greek philosophy on the substance of Roman law is extremely slight.[9]

[5] F. Schulz, *Roman Legal Science* (Oxford, 1946), pp. 38ff.

[6] For a bibliography of the question see Watson, *Law Making*, p. 187, n. 4.

[7] Cf. A. Watson, *The Law of Obligations in the Later Roman Republic* (Oxford, 1965), pp. 46ff; for a different approach, see now G. MacCormack, 'A Note on *Arra* in Plautus', *Irish Jurist*, vi (1971), pp. 361ff.

[8] Few scholars would place the introduction of consensual sale much later than the middle of the 2nd century B.C. I consider it an invention of the late 3rd century B.C.

[9] The only texts which might be thought to show there was some influence are D. 33. 10. 7. 2 (Celsus *19 dig.*); 50. 16. 25. 1 (Paul *21 ad ed.*); 5. 1. 78 (Alfenus

Likewise it can scarcely be argued that the general systematisation of Roman law in this period owed much to Greek models. Apart from anything else, Roman law was just not arranged in any logical system. This appears both from the order of the Praetor's Edict[10] and from juristic books.[11] At the most, Greek influence on systematisation may be found in the division of topics. Quintus Mucius, the consul of 95 B.C., is said to have been the first to arrange the civil law *generatim*.[12] He also distinguished five *genera* of tutorship,[13] and different *genera* of possession.[14] Servius Sulpicius, the consul of 51 B.C., distinguished three *genera* of tutorship[15] and four *genera* of theft.[16] *Genus* here corresponds to the Greek philosophical term γένος, but there is no sign in Republican juristic remains of the subdivision of a *genus* into *species*, εἶδος.[17] This is the more striking because this subdivision is prominent in Cicero's rhetorical work, *Topica*.[18]

Thus, Greek influence on Roman law in the Hellenistic period is slight. It is scarcely, if at all, to be found in substantive law; not to be found in a major arrangement of the system though probably, but to a limited extent, in divisions into *genera*.

The conclusion to be drawn from all this is that it is perfectly possible for a powerful legal system to be developed by native talent without the help of transplants, and, more surprisingly, that this can happen even in a community which in general is adopting much of another civilisation. It should not be thought, though, that a great

---

6 *dig.*). For the very limited significance of these see F. Horak, *Rationes decidendi*, i (Aalen, 1969), pp. 224ff and 230; Watson, *Law Making*, pp. 123f and 188ff.

[10] This can be largely reconstructed for the age of Hadrian; cf. O. Lenel, *Das Edictum Perpetuum*, 3rd edit. (Leipzig, 1927) pp. xviff. And there is every reason to think that the arrangement in the Republic was no better.

[11] See the reconstruction of these in O. Lenel, *Palingenesia Iuris Civilis*, i, ii (Leipzig, 1889). The 'true dialectical system' which Schulz (*Roman Legal Science* (Oxford, 1946), p. 95) finds in Quintus Mucius' *Ius civile* just does not correspond to the arrangement of the fragments; cf. Watson, *Law Making*, pp. 143ff.

[12] D. 1. 2. 2. 41 (Pomponius *sing enchir.*).

[13] G. 1. 188.

[14] D. 41. 2. 3. 23 (Paul 54 *ad ed.*)

[15] G. 1. 188.   [16] G. 3. 183.

[17] It is a matter for doubt whether Quintus Mucius wrote a *liber singularis* ὅρων (book of Definitions); see now A. Watson, *The Law of Property in the Later Roman Republic* (Oxford, 1969), p. 190: A. Rodger, 'Roman Rain-Water', *T.v.R.* xxxviii (1970), pp. 417ff at p. 426.

[18] E.g. at 7. 30 where Cicero explains that he prefers to translate εἶδος by *forma* rather than *species*.

period of legal development and legal confidence is necessarily a time of little borrowing: the example of England in the early Middle Ages when much was taken from Rome is against that idea.[19]

A country whose laws are largely derivative may itself show great originality at times. Thus the Scottish Act, c.45 of 1424 was the earliest statute in Europe to introduce free legal aid for the poor in civil cases.[20]

---

[19] See J. L. Barton, *Roman Law in England*, part 5.13b of *Ius romanum medii aevi* (Milan, 1971).

[20] Cf. J. N. Young, 'Legal Aid in Scotland', *Alabama Law Review*, xxi (1969), pp. 191ff.

CHAPTER 13

LEX AQUILIA: RECEPTION AND NON-RECEPTION

Mention has been made before of the Roman *lex Aquilia*, the statute which was mainly concerned with damage to property.[1] In the Middle Ages, in the Renaissance and in 17th-century Holland it was not doubted, so far as I am aware, that the *lex* had been received in Western Europe. At the present time what is called the Aquilian action is still the standard South African remedy for most delictal offences which involve financial loss.[2] And in fact, given the extent to which discussion of the *lex Aquilia*, even of minor points, has been relevant for subsequent lawyers,[3] it must be accepted that there has been a reception of the statute.[4] Yet doubts have been forcefully expressed. The famous German jurist, Christianus Thomasius (1655–1728) published a thesis at Magdeburg in 1728 entitled *Larva legis Aquiliae detracta actioni de damno dato, receptae in foris Germanorum* – 'The Ghost of the Lex Aquilia removed from the Action on Inflicted Loss Accepted in the Courts of the Germans'. In this work he claims that the action in Germany *de damno dato* was as different from the *lex Aquilia* as a bird from a quadruped. First he gives his opinion on what the *ius gentium* on the subject would be. Then he demonstrates that this is very different from the provisions of the *lex Aquilia*. Next he shows that the law in use is vastly different from the Roman statute and argues that the *lex* was therefore never received. And finally he puts

[1] Supra, pp. 27ff, 58ff.

[2] Cf. e.g., R. G. McKerron, *The Law of Delict*, 7th edit. (Cape Town, 1971), pp. 13ff; *Maasdorp's Institutes of South African Law*, iv, 8th edit., by C. G. Hall (Cape Town, 1972), passim.

[3] For a few modern instances see the South African cases of *Van Tonder* v. *Alexander*, 1906 E.D.L. 186; *Daly* v. *Chisholm*, 1916 C.P.D. 562; *Transvaal and Rhodesian Estates Ltd.* v. *Golding*, 1917 A.D. 184; *Oslo Land Company Ltd.* v. *The Union Government*, 1938 A.D. 584; *Gillespie* v. *Toplis & Another*, 1951 (1) S.A. 290; *Rohloff* v. *Ocean Accident and Guarantee Corpn. Ltd.*, 1960 (2) S.A. 291. In not all of these are the rules of the *lex Aquilia* followed, but it is the fact of the present-day discussion which best shows the reception.

[4] Cf., e.g., F. P. van den Heever, *Aquilian Damages in South African Law*, i (Cape Town, N.D.).

up a plea for the acceptance of the dictates of the *ius gentium* in these points where it differs from the law accepted in Germany.

Thomasius is vigorously supported by J. G. Heineccius (1681–1741) who summarises the points where *hodiernum ius* differs from the *lex Aquilia* in his *Recitationes in Elementa Iuris Civilis*, 4. 3 § MXCV iiii: 'Fourthly, it remains for us to look into the present use of this title. And here indeed the Doctors commonly praise the use of this action in a marvellous manner. But if you calculate properly, you will scarcely ever find it in court. There is in this land an action on account of loss inflicted, for recovering loss and for exacting a penalty. But that is also so among the Turks and the Chinese who never took anything from Roman law. But, I ask you, do we today distinguish slaves and four-footed herd animals from all other things? And do we estimate the highest value which the thing had within a year or thirty days? And do we ask in a subtle manner, whether the loss was inflicted by the body to the body, or by the body but not to the body, or neither by the body nor to the body? And finally is the sum of damages doubled here if liability is denied? Of course, no one would say that. And who therefore can say that the action under the *lex Aquilia* has been received? Therefore the present action for inflicted loss truly comes from natural law and our national statutes, not from the *lex Aquilia*.'[5]

Heineccius is right to give a negative reply to the four (really rhetorical) questions in the middle of the quotation. Yet Chapter 1 of the Roman *lex Aquilia* covered only the killing of slaves and herd animals and gave as damages the highest value the slave or animal had in the past year, Chapter 3 dealt with all other injuries and the action was for the loss which became apparent within thirty days of the injury.[6] In the Empire the statute was interpreted restrictively as

[5] '*Quarto superest, ut de usu huius tituli hodierno disquiramus. Et hic quidem doctores vulgo mirifice celebrant huius actionis usum. Sed si calculum recte ponas, nullum fere in foro deprehendes. Agitur quidem apud nos de damno dato: agitur ad damnum resarciendum, poenamque persolvendam. Sed id etiam apud Turcas et Sinenses fit, qui numquam ex iure Romano quidquam receperunt. Sed, quaeso, an et nos hodie distinguimus servos et pecudes quadrupedes a reliquis rebus? An et nos aestimamus res, quanti intra annum vel 30 dies plurimi fuere? An et apud nos quaeritur subtiliter, sitne damnum corpore corpori, an corpore sed non corpori, an nec corpore nec corpori datum? An denique et apud nos lis infitiando crescit? Nemo sane hoc dixerit. Et qui dici ergo potest, actionem ex L. Aquillia esse receptam? Est ergo hodierna actio de damno dato vere ex iure naturali et statutis patriis, non ex L. Aquillia.*'

[6] The meaning of the 30 days' clause is disputed, but this is to accept the view of D. Daube; cf. now his *Roman Law; Linguistic, Social and Philosophical Aspects*

covering only injuries directly caused – in later terminology, 'by the body to the body' – and analogous actions were given for indirect damage. For all three chapters of the *lex*, the measure of damages was doubled if the defendant denied liability.

Thus, in fact, despite the importance of the *lex Aquilia* – especially the discussions of negligence – for subsequent generations and its prominence in post-Roman legal writings, its special features were not taken over by the mediaeval or renaissance lawyers.[7] We have to beware of exaggerating the extent of a transplant. Here, as in some other cases, what is adopted is mainly the terminology;[8] and the substance of the law remains largely unchanged though it has become more sophisticated.

(Edinburgh, 1969), pp. 66ff. In post-Roman times the clause was generally understood as having meant that the plaintiff was to get the highest value the thing had had in the 30 days prior to the injury.

[7] This development is very different from that of the action for personal disfigurement where the Roman rule was first accepted and gradually modified; see supra, pp. 27ff. This time the peculiar Roman rules were not really accepted at all.

[8] For other suggested instances where what is borrowed is mainly the terminology, see B. S. Jackson, 'Evolution and Foreign Influence in Ancient Law', *American Journal of Comparative Law*, xvi (1968), pp. 372ff at pp. 375f and n. 17.

CHAPTER 14

TRANSFER OF OWNERSHIP AND RISK IN SALE

When an institution is completely received it none the less seems almost inevitable that differences will occur even when they are not dictated by social change and progress, and even when the old rule can still be regarded as satisfactory and the new one has no overwhelming claim to succeed.

Perhaps the single Roman legal institution which has been most acceptable and least changed right up to the present day is the contract of sale, *emptio venditio*. It is worthy of note that the idea of consensual contracts – contracts which require no formalities but which depend for their validity solely upon the agreement of the parties – is purely a Roman invention, and that in all probability the first consensual contract was *emptio venditio*. But modern sale has variations on the Roman contract.

One of the most interesting of these concerns the transfer of risk and ownership. At Rome, risk of damage or destruction passed as a rule to the buyer as soon as the sale became perfect, which in the normal case would be the moment of agreement.[1] Ownership, though, again as a rule, passed to the buyer only when the thing was actually delivered.[2] But in the French *Code civil*, risk and ownership pass together to the buyer as soon as the contract is perfect.[3] In the German *Bürgerliches Gesetzbuch*, risk and ownership pass together to the buyer but only on delivery of the thing.[4] Swiss law follows Roman and risk passes to the buyer when the contract is perfect,[5] but ownership is transferred only with delivery.[6]

What the Roman law was on the subject was perfectly clear, though

---

[1] Cf., e.g., 18. 6. 8 (Paul *33 ad ed.*) D. 18. 1. 35. 4 (Gaius *10 ad ed. prov.*); 19. 1. 31 pr. (Neratius *3 membr.*).

[2] Cf., e.g., G. 2. 19; D. 41. 1. 9. 3, 4, 5 (Gaius *2 rer. cott.*) For certain important things before Justinian a formal ceremony, *mancipatio*, was needed.

[3] Art. 1138, 1583–7, 1624.

[4] §§ 446, 929.

[5] *Schweizerisches Obligationenrecht*, 185.

[6] *Schweizerisches Zivilgesetzbuch*, 714; cf. 922.

complicated by questions of the seller's negligence and of his delay
in delivering, and of the buyer's delay in accepting delivery. Before the
Code civil the Roman rules were generally accepted in France[7] and the
law is so stated by Pothier.[8] This was also the law accepted by the first
modern European code, the Prussian *Allgemeines Landrecht für die
Preussischen Staaten* of 1794.[9] An examination of writings on Roman
and later national law before the *Code civil* confirms that this was the
general approach.

There were, though, occasional voices raised in disagreement. The
great Cuiacius (1522(?)–1590), for example, argued on the basis of
D. 19. 2. 33 (Africanus *8 quaest.*) that the Romans did regard the risk
as remaining with the seller before delivery.[10] He also declares that this
is the more equitable opinion: 'And, indeed, it is fairer that a buyer
who has not acquired the thing does not pay the price.'[11] But elsewhere
the same jurist, discussing D. 18. 1. 34. 5 (Paul *33 ad ed.*), observes that
after a sale becomes perfect, the thing sold is at the risk of the buyer.[12]

Probably more significant for the later development were the 17th
century writers on Natural law. Hugo Grotius (1583–1645) in his *De
Jure Belli Ac Pacis* (first published in Paris, 1625) says that with regard
to sale ownership may be transferred, without delivery, at the moment
of contract, and that this is the simplest approach. He cites Seneca in
support; and observes that Theophrastus holds that most legislators
have provided that both benefit and risk are on the seller until delivery.[13] Pufendorf's (1632–1694) treatment of the same topic in his *De
Jure Naturae et Gentium* (first published in Lund, 1672) is more satisfactory. He correctly states the Roman law without equivocation, and
then seeks what he calls 'natural equity'. He distinguishes three cases:
where the delay is necessary for the delivery; where it is due to the
slowness of the seller; and where it is due to the slowness of the buyer.[14]
The last two cases, like the Roman rules on *mora*, need not concern us.
But in the first case Pufendorf declares 'there is no doubt that reason
orders the loss to fall upon the seller'.[15] Thus, he makes risk and

---

[7] Cf., e.g., R.-Th. Troplong, *Le Droit civil, De la vente*, 4th edit. (Paris, 1845),
p. 476.

[8] *Traité du contrat de vente* (first published, Paris, 1762) §§ 307, 318.

[9] I. 10. I; I. 11. 95, 96.

[10] *Tractatus ad Africanum*, VIII.

[11] 'Et vero aequius est, ut qui rem non est nactus emptor, pretium non solvat.'

[12] *Recitationes solemnes in libros Pauli ad Edictum.*

[13] 2. 12. 15.   [14] 5. 5. 3.

[15] 'Heic quin ratio jubeat damnum esse venditoris, dubium non est.'

ownership pass together, but at delivery. The lesser known Jean Barbeyrac (1674–1744), a Huguenot who left France after the revocation of the Edict of Nantes in 1685 and taught successively at the Universities of Berlin, Lausanne and Groningen, editor of Grotius' *De Jure Belli ac Pacis*, editor and translator into French of Pufendorf's *De Jure Naturae et Gentium*, took the view that the best solution was to make ownership and risk pass together at the moment of agreement, and he criticised the wrongheadedness of the Romans in requiring physical delivery for the transfer of ownership.[16]

Although there is no direct evidence it is plausible to assert that Cuiacius and Grotius, more particularly Pufendorf, and above all Barbeyrac were responsible for the rule in the *Code civil*. As usual, the compilers of the *Code* will have studied Pothier who refers to the divergent views of Cuiacius, Pufendorf and Barbeyrac.[17] Troplong in his commentary (which was first published in 1834) on the sale provisions of the *Code* observes that the Roman law was judged to be contrary to natural law by Pufendorf and Barbeyrac, and above all by Grotius whose authority is much weightier, and he also mentions the view of Cuiacius.[18] The repetition here of Pufendorf, Barbeyrac and Cuiacius, this time with approval, after their appearance in Pothier, strongly suggests that they were thought influential in the formation of the *Code* rules, the emphasis on Natural law stresses the contribution of Pufendorf and Barbeyrac, and it was, of course, the opinion held by this last which actually was accepted.

Strangely, in an earlier work, the *Elementa Jurisprudentiae Universalis* (first published at the Hague in 1660), Pufendorf expressed himself vigorously in favour of the moral rightness of risk passing to the buyer as soon as agreement was reached though ownership remained with the seller until delivery.[19] And Grotius in his work on the law of

[16] Thus, he says in his note on Pufendorf, 5. 5. 3., 'Les Jurisconsultes Romains, et leurs Interprètes, auroient évité tous ces embarras, et établi des principes mieux liez, s'ils ne s'étoient entêtez d'une fausse idée du transport de Propriété, qu'ils prétendent ne pouvoir se faire que par une prise de possession corporelle.'

[17] *Contrat de vente*, § 307.

[18] Chap. IV, § 358. In the 4th edit., pp. 475f.

[19] 1. 12. 56. '*Quod si vis contractus non expresse a traditione rei suspendatur, sed pure contractum ac jus ad rem emptori fuerit datum, statim ut in pretium modumque solvendi fuit consensum, periculum rei ad emptorem pertinet, nisi dolus venditoris intervenerit. Nam cum statim traditionem rei venditor emptori praestare hoc casu debuerit, imputet sibi emptor, si dum moram interponit, detrimenti quid res sua passa fuerit. Nec obstat, quod alias dicatur res domino suo perire; heic autem a venditore rei venditae dominum nondum videatur transisse ad emptorem, non facta traditone. Nam pro domino amplius*

Holland, *Inleiding tot de Hollandsche Rechtsgeleertheyd* (written between 1619 and 1621, first published at the Hague in 1631) simply declares that on perfection of the contract, although the buyer is not yet owner, risk passes to him.[20]

It may be, as F. H. Lawson suggests,[21] that the customs of northern France had helped to create a favourable atmosphere for the rules adopted in the *Code civil*. For the so-called *clause de dessaisine-saisine*, a clause which (falsely) declared that delivery had taken place, was sufficient to effect the transfer of ownership.[22] Of course, this type of transfer of ownership without delivery operated only when the parties actually agreed that it should, when the contract was in writing, and apparently when the sale was of immoveables. Hence it was very different from that in the *Code civil*, which occurred automatically when the contract of sale was agreed.

The rules in the *Code civil* on the transfer of ownership and risk are, without doubt, very neat. But the German provisions of the *Bürgerliches Gesetzbuch* of 1900, almost a century after the *Code civil*, show that they were not the only practical alternative to the Roman rules. One might also feel, indeed, that the German approach is more logical. And the Swiss provisions of the *Schweizerisches Gesetzbuch* of 1907 and the *Schweizerisches Obligationenrecht* of 1911 show that the Roman rules could be regarded as having a fundamental usefulness even by people who were well aware of other solutions and of how these were working in practice. In other words, the French rejection of the Roman rules on this point was not the result of social development, nor due to inherent practical weaknesses of the older system nor the consequence of an awareness of the logical necessity of their own preferred view.

In legal development there is, of course, no such thing as pure chance. No doubt particular and immediate historical reasons exist

---

agnosci non potest, intra cujus spatia res adhuc aliqua est non jure aliquo, sed mero emptoris arbitrio, quam quandocunque postulaverit, statim concedere tenetur, nulla interea isti circa eam disponendi facultate relicta.'

[20] 3. 14. 34. '*De koop van eenige zaken voltrocken zijnde sulcs als vooren is gheseit, hoe-wel den kooper noch gheen eigenaer en is, ende noch geen levering en is geschied, so staet de saecke tot baet ende schade van den kooper, oversulcks sullen den kooper van dien tijd af volghen alle vruchten, oock aenwas van land, wederom indien 't verkochte goed vergaet ofte verargert, sulcs komt tot des koopers schade.*'

[21] *A Common Lawyer Looks at the Civil Law* (Ann Arbor, 1953), p. 170.

[22] Cf. E. Chenon, *Histoire générale du droit français public et privé*, ii (Paris, 1929), pp. 219.

not only for the French change but also for the different German and
Swiss rules. But when that is said it must also be admitted that neither
in France nor in Germany[23] was there a general historical movement
away from the Roman provisions on the transfer of ownership and
risk.[24] Nor were there social, political, commercial or geographical
conditions in France which made the Roman rules inappropriate; nor
in Germany to make the French rules disagreeable; nor in Switzerland
to make the French and German rules less suitable than the Roman
ones. One could not possibly maintain that the differences here reflect
the different 'Volksgeist'. A plain man would, on reflection, conclude
that chance had played an important role.

A critique of Savigny's 'Volksgeist' theory[25] is not at all to the purpose of this book. But the last paragraph demands that a little more
be said. Savigny maintains that as civilisation progresses the activities
of the people become more and more separate and what was once
done in common becomes the preserve of particular classes. At this
stage the jurists too appear a separate class. Law takes a scientific
direction, and just as previously it lived in the common consciousness
of the people, so now, he says, it is proper to the consciousness of the
jurists who in this respect now represent the people. Law is then more
complex and artificial since it has a double life, once as part of the life
of the whole people, which it does not cease to be, and then as a special
science in the hands of the jurists. All the later developments are
explained by the concurrence of this double life-principle, and it
becomes understandable how such immense detail can arise in an
organic manner without real arbitrariness and intent.[26] Now if this
means, as it must, something more than the truism that in a developed
society the details of law are worked out by the lawyers, the argument
must be that legal details come from the common consciousness of the
legal profession who represent, at one remove, the common consciousness of the people. Hence the detail must correspond, first, to the
historical and social trend among the lawyers, and secondly, in a more

[23] For various distinguished German explanations and justifications for the
Roman rule see the authorities cited and discussed by H. Dernburg, *Pandekten*,
ii, 7th edit. (Berlin, 1903), p. 264, n. 3.

[24] Before the compilation of the *B.G.B.* there was a great academic dispute
between the German Romanists and the Germanists, the latter wanting a general
return to Germanic law. The *B.G.B.* was a victory for the Romanists.

[25] Cf. supra, pp. 21f.

[26] *Vom Beruf unsrer Zeit für Gesetzgebung und Rechtswissenschaft* (Heidelberg,
1814), p. 12.

general way, to the spirit of the people. Or, given the people's ignorance of legal detail, it must not be contrary to what the people think the law is or should be. And I would maintain first that there was no general historical or social trend among French, German and Swiss lawyers towards the particular rules which were adopted in their countries on the transfer of ownership and risk in sale. And secondly, that most people in these countries, then and now, believe both that ownership and risk are transferred to the buyer at the moment of delivery, and that that is the way it should be whatever lawyers and courts say to the contrary.[27, 28]

To end this chapter with a more speculative point. If it was correct to suggest that the main source of these provisions of the *Code civil* was the opinions of Pufendorf and Barbeyrac, then it is possible that the provisions are directly due to the writings of Pothier. By disagreeing with Pufendorf and Barbeyrac, Pothier – the jurist whose work had most influence on the formation of the *Code* – called attention to views which might have been overlooked by the compilers since the great weight of authority was on the side of the Roman rules.

[27] D. Daube points out that in no system is any loss before delivery divided between seller and buyer; 'The Scales of Justice', *J.R.*, lxviii (1951) pp. 109ff at p. 110.

[28] Actually the 'Volksgeist' theory has been amply refuted by numerous jurists, but it lives on – and will continue to do so – because of its immediate emotional appeal.

CHAPTER 15

AUTHORITY AGAIN

Several times before in this book, the importance of authority in the process of transplanting has been stressed. I should like to return for a moment, irrelevantly some may feel, to two other, very different, aspects of authority.

It would, I suppose, be unreasonable to regard as transplants laws given by gods to men. But Yahweh directly gave the Ten Commandments to Moses on Mount Sinai.[1] Apollo, through the Delphic oracle, gave Lycurgus the laws of Sparta,[2] Zeus gave the Cretans their laws,[3] and Hermes gave the Egyptians theirs through Mneves.[4] The significance for us of these traditions is that the fiction of a gift of god heightens the laws' authority and makes their acceptance and maintenance easier. As Plutarch says: 'Thus the law code of Zaleucus found favour with the Locrians not least, it is said, because he asserted that Athena had constantly appeared to him and had in each case guided and instructed him in his legislation, and that nothing he proposed was of his own invention or devising.'[5] Nothing could illustrate better man's need to have his laws as authoritative as possible in order to ensure that they are obeyed.[6]

Secondly, it is striking how often codifications are produced for, or demanded by, national heroes, despots, and military leaders. Thus, the king Lipit-Ishtar who 'procured the freedom of the sons and daughters

---

[1] Exodus 20; Deuteronomy 5. Probably within biblical times the whole pentateuch was regarded as so given.

[2] Cf., e.g., Herodotus, *Historiae*, 1. 65; Plutarch, *Lycurgus*, 5. 3; Plato, *Laws*, 1 (p. 624); Diodorus Siculus, 1. 94.

[3] Plato, *Laws*, 1 (p. 624); Diodorus Siculus, 1. 94.

[4] Diodorus Siculus, 1. 94.

[5] *De se ipsum citra invidiam laudando*, 11: cf. scholiast in Pindar, *Olymp*. 10. 17. See also for the laws of Numa in regal Rome, Dionysius of Halicarnassus, 2. 61.

[6] See also, H. H. Cohn, 'Secularization of Divine Law', *Scripta Hierosolymitana*, xvi (Jerusalem, 1966), pp. 55ff.

of Nippur, the sons and daughters of Ur, the sons and daughters of Isin, the sons and daughters of Sumer and Akkad upon whom slaveship had been imposed'[7] is the king responsible for one of the earliest known legal codes, probably of the early 19th century B.C. And Hammurabi, king of Babylon in the 18th century B.C., is as famous for his conquests as for his code. Moses, who led his people out of bondage in Egypt, also acquired for them the Ten Commandments. Both Julius Caesar[8] and Pompey the Great[9] wished to codify the law of Rome. Justinian, who did so successfully from Constantinople between A.D. 529 and 534, also reconquered Africa, Italy and part of southern Spain. In more recent times, the impetus for the first modern European codification, Prussia's *Allgemeines Landrecht*, came from Frederick the Great, and Napoleon was responsible for the *Code civil*. The phenomenon is complex and has several causes, one of which is the conqueror's desire to be remembered as a wise man of peace since a main benefit of peace is law and justice. There is also the wish to be the initiator of a new era. Another cause is undoubtedly the man of action's impatience with the convolutions and ambiguities which invade any legal system, and especially one which has developed without overall planning. What *he* wants is a system which is its own authority, one in which an answer to every problem exists, and can be quickly found by the interested parties. The speed and certainty of the answer is more important to *him* than its subtlety or absolute quality.[10] There is a link here with transplants which owe much of their popularity to the ease with which the rule can be acquired even when it is not wholly appropriate in its adoptive society.

The central rôle in law of authority – as contrasted with quality – is thus emphasised.[11] Law should be its own authority; for some people (including legislators) it has sometimes seemed more important that

---

[7] From the prologue of the Lipit-Ishtar Law code, translated by S. N. Kramer in J. B. Pritchard, *Ancient Near Eastern Texts Relating to the Old Testament*, 3rd edit. (Princeton, 1969), pp. 159ff.

[8] Cf. Suetonius, *Divus Iulius*, 44. 2; Isidorus, *Orig.* 5. 1. 5.

[9] Cf. Isidorus, *Orig.* 5. 1. 5.

[10] Some of these leaders, notably Napoleon and Frederick the Great, were extremely interested in the quality of the rules of their codification. But always they wanted a decision made as to what the law on a point was; and always they wished to end discussion, controversy and doubt.

[11] On the significance and effects of an authoritative tradition see, e.g., M. P. Gilmore, *Argument from Roman Law in Political Thought 1200–1600* (Cambridge, Mass., 1941).

the law be easily known than that it have objectively excellent rules.[12]
Again a law is often adopted because of the reputation and authority
of its model or promulgator; hence, in part, the reception of even
less than adequate rules. Finally, law is maintained by the authority of
the government, and even gods are invoked; questioning, examining
of quality is reduced to a poor second best.

The Western world has, of course, been completely brain-washed
by the authority of Roman law, especially as the law was set forth
in Justinian's *Corpus Juris Civilis*. The main divisions of the law, the
major institutions, the boundary lines between one institution and
another – all as fixed by the Romans – are so ingrained in us that we
find it very difficult to conceive of the possibility of other arrangements.
Yet a moment's glance at other systems will show us that Roman rules
are not inevitably the only ones.

Thus in the 4th century B.C., a great period of Athens, Attic law
does not divide into private and public law. Marriage was so different
from our concept that it is difficult to establish the precise meaning of
ἐγγύη, the most important term. It was not a completed marriage,
but probably the arrangement which became marriage – possibly
years later – when the union was consummated. Ἐγγύη was apparently
not essential for all marriages. Ἐπιδικασία was the procedure for the
marriage of an ἐπίκληρος, 'heiress': when a man died leaving no son
but only a daughter, the right to her hand went in a prescribed order
to the nearest male relative. If this daughter was already married the
nearest male relative, if he wished to marry her, could have her
marriage dissolved. The penalty which could be inflicted on a man for
raping a married woman was less than the penalty which could be
inflicted upon him for seducing a married woman. Marriage between
brother and sister who had the same father but a different mother was
permitted. Indeed, one of the standard methods of adoption was for a
man who had only a daughter to adopt a son who was to marry her;
and in fact it appears that such a man could adopt a son only for marriage with the daughter. If a man died intestate it would seem that
ascendants were totally excluded from the inheritance. Only a man
of full age could make a will, and then, strictly only of he had no
legitimate sons; if he had no sons but only daughters he could dispose of
his property by marrying them to men whom he adopted. In the law

---

[12] Cf. the Roman tradition of the plebs' demand in the 5th century B.C. for codification – which led to the XII Tables – because they did not know what the law
was: Livy, 3.9. 1ff.

of property, we find there was no real juristic classification of things, derivative modes of acquisition of property were not clearly separated from the transactions at the root of the transfer, acquisition of ownership by prescription did not really exist, and though the distinction between ownership and possession was recognised no system was developed to protect the two different rights.[13]

One could find equally wide divergences from Roman and modern Western classification in, say, classical Islamic law where sale is an exchange of goods and hence includes barter, money-changing is sale of price for price, while hire is the sale of a usufruct.[14]

The approach of modern law reform bodies also raises questions of borrowing and authority. No doubt each of these bodies has its own methods, but it will be enough to look briefly at one. When the Scottish Law Commission considers any question of major reform the first instinct is to look at solutions in other jurisdictions. Indeed, the Law Commissions of both Scotland and England are by statute required to take account of the solutions of foreign systems of law and to consult with each other.[15] But there is no set procedure in Scotland and no one country's law is thought to have more weight than another's. In the normal case the law of England is looked at first, though not, I have been told, because it is thought to have special authority. There are, of course, great advantages in having the laws of Scotland and England the same. If a problem which raises similar social problems in England is under consideration, the Commissioners (of both countries) will probably seek harmonisation or unification of solutions. Thereafter, for Scotland there are three main possibilities. One is that the law of certain commonwealth countries will be considered, if it is known that there have been recent and significant developments. Thus, Australian, Canadian and New Zealand law – as well as that of England – was looked at in connection with divorce. Secondly, the work of the legal committees of the Council of Europe

---

[13] Many of the statements made here are disputed by various scholars. See above all, A. R. W. Harrison, *The Law of Athens*, i, *The Family and Property* (Oxford, 1968), ii, *Procedure* (Oxford, 1971) with full citation of sources. The main earlier general works are L. Beauchet, *L'Histoire du droit privé de la République Athénienne* (Paris, 1897); J. H. Lipsius, *Das attische Recht und Rechtsverfahren* (reprinted Darmstadt, 1966).

[14] Cf., e.g., J. Schacht, *Introduction to Islamic Law* (Oxford, 1964), pp. 152, 154. Interestingly, there are indications that in the early 2nd century B.C. at Rome the line between sale and hire was not always drawn precisely as it was later: Cato, *De agri cultura*, 149, 150.   [15] Law Commissions Act 1965, ss. 3. i. f, 3. iv.

and of Unidroit is regarded as important as an indication of European trends; and the laws of European countries most often referred to are those of, first, France and than Germany. Continental systems had considerable influence on the conceptual structure for reform of the law on capacity for legal acts and for acquiring property rights. Little attention is directed towards Dutch law primarily because none of the Commissioners reads Dutch, though they have access to the unofficial English translation of Meijer's Draft Code for Holland so far as it has progressed.[16] Roman-Dutch law should perhaps also be mentioned here since it is regarded as important for contract, delict and moveable property. The third likely approach is to think of the law of Scandinavian countries. Scots law is different in its principles from the law there, but social conditions are often very similar, particularly in the areas of low population density. Thus, the law of Finland, the Scandinavian countries, Western Australia and Upper Canada formed the basis for comparison in the method of enforcing payment of judgment debts in sparsely populated areas. In general, little use is made of the possibility of comparison with Soviet law or the law of the United States. The former is based on different social premises. The lack of influence of the latter is more interesting and has, I think, two main causes. First the very multiplicity of American solutions may well daunt the Commissioners. Secondly, this same multiplicity demands, if American law is to be used seriously, the existence of a large and extensive collection of the relevant books such as just does not exist in Scotland. The Commissioners have, however, used the American Model Code of Evidence and the Restatements of agency, contract and tort.

Thus in this case (and in others), a body set up to suggest law reforms begins normally not by trying to think its way through to its own solution based on local conditions and character but by examining external solutions. There is a conscious attempt to achieve the best possible rule. But the process is not entirely free from chance. Non-legal factors – library and linguistic deficiences – reduce the rôle which might be played by certain systems. It should be noted that neither the Commissioners nor the Commission's legal staff are selected primarily because of their experience in Comparative Law or their linguistic skills.[17]

[16] They can, of course, have material translated.

[17] Much information is, of course, received on legal developments in other iurisdictions.

It is obvious that if books are not available in libraries or if they are written in a language which is not understood, the law in them will not be directly influential. Further, books in a language which is not commonly known tend not to be bought by libraries, hence cannot be used even by those few persons capable of reading them, and so their potential influence is even more diminished. Edinburgh University's splendid Centre for European Government Studies does not contain the Dutch Parliamentary Reports.

Clearly, one factor in the widespread reception of Roman law was that what later came to be called the *Corpus Juris Civilis* was written in Latin, a language understood by all educated men in Europe for many centuries. Those parts of the *Corpus* which were written in Greek were not lectured on – *Graeca non leguntur* – and comments on them are sparse in the Middle Ages. Similarly, later, of the work of two Scotsmen, Craig's *Ius Feudale* was influential in Europe (and was reprinted in Leipzig in 1716): Stair's *Institutions of the Law of Scotland* was not.

Another factor was that the *Corpus Juris* provided a *written* system which was detailed yet was in not too great a bulk. Law which is not written has far less chance of spreading. It has in fact been argued that English law[18] is incapable of being received – in distinction to being imposed or having individual institutions accepted – and one reason for this belief is that English law is 'jurists' law', *Juristenrecht*, and not contained in something approaching a code.[19] But in America there was a true reception of the Common law in almost all of the States which were never colonies of England.[20, 21] What must not be forgotten is that there is no need for the primary instrument of the reception to be the law of the donor state in its official form.[22] After the Revolution, the Civil law had many adherents in America,[23] but it failed to make

[18] And Anglo-American law in general.

[19] Cf., e.g., A. Kocourek, 'Factors in the Reception of Law', *Studi Albertoni*, iii (Padua, 1938), pp. 251ff; P. Koschaker, *Europa und das römische Recht*, 2nd edit. (Munich, Berlin, 1953), pp. 161f.

[20] Cf., e.g., J. N. Hazard, 'Problems of Reception in the United States', *Annales de la Faculté de Droit de l'Université d'Istambul*, v (1956), pp. 217ff.

[21] Of course, it is not to be denied that political factors are very important in receptions.

[22] Witness the influence of *lo Codi*; supra, pp. 61ff.

[23] Cf., above all, Perry Miller, *The Life of the Mind in America* (London, 1966), pp. 164ff; P. Stein, 'The Attraction of the Civil Law in Post-Revolutionary America', *Virginia Law Review*, lii (1966), pp. 403ff.

much permanent impact. The victory of the Common law would, I suggest, have been much more difficult and perhaps even impossible had it not been for Blackstone's *Commentaries on the Laws of England*. The authority and popularity of this four-volume work was enormous. In his lifetime it ran through eight editions in England, the ninth was ready at his death in 1780, and it made its author a small fortune. At least 21 'straight' English editions were published in America from 1771–1774; from 1803 onwards, at least 94 editions emerged with American notes; and there were at least 55 editions of abridgements for students, including the *Pennsylvania Blackstone* by J. Reed (1871), and the extremely popular *American Student's Blackstone*.[24] The work covered all the law, and in American editions was usually printed in two volumes. Thus, it was comprehensive, cheap, and convenient for slipping into saddle bags – an ideal work in fact for sparsely populated areas.[25]

[24] These figures ignore Canadian editions.

[25] T. B. Smith is wrong when he claims 'None, it may be added, outside England have been voluntary converts to her [i.e. 'Our Lady of the Common Law] worship': 'Scottish Nationalism, Law and Self-Government', *The Scottish Debate*, edit. by N. MacCormick (London, 1970), pp. 34ff at p. 36.

CHAPTER 16

SOME GENERAL REFLECTIONS

Any discussion of legal borrowings and relationships could continue interminably, but we are now in a position, I think, to offer a few general reflections, which will be arranged in the order of the most obvious proceeding to the less obvious.

First, the transplanting of individual rules or of a large part of a legal system is extremely common. This is true both of early times – witness the ancient Near East – and the present day.

Secondly, transplanting is, in fact, the most fertile source of development. Most changes in most systems are the result of borrowing. This is so both for individual rules and for systematics as can be seen in the overwhelming importance for the Western world's private law of Roman Civil law and English Common law. Of his own country's system G. Tedeschi writes:[1] 'In the Law of the State of Israel the foreign elements predominate, and their foreign origin is obvious and unmistakable. This is the case to such an extent that in most spheres it is difficult to point to any significant contribution of our own.' A similar predominance, even if not always so obvious, exists in other systems. Consequently, Comparative Law and a knowledge of foreign and out-of-state law would seem to be of fundamental importance for legal progress.

Thirdly, to a truly astounding degree law is rooted in the past. 'The forms of action we have buried,' says F. W. Maitland,[2] 'but they still rule us from their graves.' The dictum could be generalised. For example, the contract of sale in the whole Western world, Common law countries and Civil law countries alike, is fundamentally that which existed at Rome in the later 2nd century A.D. Incredibly, what is contained in a modern Civil Code depends primarily upon the contents of the *Institutes* of Justinian of the year A.D. 533.

Fourthly, the transplanting of legal rules is socially easy. Whatever opposition there might be from the bar or legislature, it remains true that legal rules move easily and are accepted into the system without

[1] 'On Reception and on the Legislative Policy of Israel', *Scripta Hierosolymitana* xvi (Jerusalem, 1966), pp. 11ff at p. 12.

[2] *Equity and The Forms of Action*, two courses of lectures edited by A. H. Chaytor and W. J. Whittaker (Cambridge, 1909), p. 296.

too great difficulty. This is so even when the rules come from a very different kind of system.[3] The truth of the matter seems to be that many legal rules make little impact on individuals, and that very often it is important that there be a rule; but what rule actually is adopted is of restricted significance for general human happiness.

It follows from the four reflections to this point that usually legal rules are not peculiarly devised for the particular society in which they now operate and also that this is not a matter for great concern.

This opinion – if it is correct – may be put to practical use especially in a time of conscious legal reform. Let me quote from a statement by a former Scottish Law Commissioner: '. . . account has necessarily to be taken of English solutions even if these are eventually rejected as unsuitable for reception into Scots law. Indeed in many contexts English solutions have to be studied to identify fundamental differences from Scots law cloaked by superficial similarity. Endeavours to achieve unified solutions in the field of Contract law have in particular revealed that what has been assumed to be common ground was approached by members of the Scottish and English Contracts Teams through conceptually opposed habits of thought. Whereas English comparative research relied particularly on American and Common-wealth sources, the background of some of the Scottish proposals derived from French, Greek, Italian and Netherlands sources – and from the Ethiopian Civil Code, which was, of course, drafted by a distinguished French comparative lawyer.'[4] Now this, to me, is rather too academic. If the *rules* of contract law of the two countries are already similar (as they are) it should be no obstacle to their unification or harmonisation that the legal *principles* involved come ultimately from different sources, or that the habits of thought of the commission teams are rather different. It is scholarly law reformers who are deeply troubled by historical factors and habits of thought. Commercial lawyers and business men in Scotland and England do not in general

[3] We are considering only the existence of similar rules and not whether they always work to similar effect in the different systems.

[4] I am grateful for permission to quote the statement. See also now the Scottish Law Commission's *Seventh Annual Report 1971–72* (Edinburgh, 1973, *Scot. Law Com.* n. 28) § 12: '. . . We view with disfavour ill-considered attempts to unify the laws of England and Scotland by the application of principles which are not consistent with Scots law . . .' The Commissioners are under a statutory duty 'to take and keep under review all the law with which they are respectively concerned with a view to its systematic development and reform . . .': Law Commissions Act, 1965, s.3.i.

perceive differences in habits of thought, but only – and often with irritation – differences in rules.

Fifthly, a voluntary reception or transplant almost always – always in the case of a major transplant – involves a change in the law, which can be due to any number of factors, such as climate, economic conditions, religious outlook – witness the Massachusetts Bay colony[5] – or even chance largely unconnected either with particular factors operating within the society as a whole or with the general historical trend. Speaking broadly though, if one were trying to discover 'the Spirit of a People' from its law one should look not to the overall system but to the details where it diverges from other systems.[6]

[But even in the details law can give many surprises. Between 1931 and 1938 Charles G. Vernier published at Stanford his five-volume work (plus supplement), *American Family Laws*. This fascinating comparative study of the law of the then forty-eight states, Alaska, District of Columbia and Hawaii gives us in a simple and tabulated form all the information which we need on state variations. Imagine an astute person well versed in the geography and history – social, racial, religious and political – of the United States but curiously ignorant of state laws, who was asked to guess, on the basis of his knowledge, which states then wholly or partially recognised common law marriage or did not recognise it, which states demanded the publication of banns of marriage, the grounds admitted for divorce in the various states, and so on. Such a person would often guess correctly but probably just as often would be wrong.]

It must also be emphasised that jurists at times exaggerate the extent of a transplant. Often the host system had a similar rule and little of importance was received apart from terminology. But even when this occurs the very use of the terminology is likely to ensure the continuing influence of the donor. A powerful example can be found in the references to Roman law in Aquilian actions in South Africa.

Some purer souls may object to the variation, the interpretation of the original, involved in major transplants. As Rabelais says of the University experiences of the noble Pantagruel: 'So from thence he

---

[5] And more recently, Turkey; cf., e.g., B. Davran, 'Bericht über die Aenderungen im türkischen ZGB gegenüber dem schweizerischen', *Annales de la Faculté de Droit d'Istambul*, v (1956), pp. 131ff.

[6] We have not expressly discussed in this book the extent to which the actual choice of a rule to be borrowed and the modifications made to it actually correspond to the needs of the society.

came to Bourges, where he studied a good long time, and profited very much in the faculty of the Lawes, and would sometimes say, that the books of the Civil Law were like unto a wonderfully precious, royal and triumphant robe of cloth of gold, edged with dirt; for in the world are no goodlier books to be seen, more ornate, nor more eloquent than the texts of the Pandects, but the bordering of them, that is to say, the glosse of Accursius is so scurvie, vile, base, and unsavourie, that it is nothing but filthinesse and villany.'[7] But the dream is unattainable.

Sixthly, no area of private law can be designated as being extremely resistant to change as a result of foreign influence. Certainly, at any rate, family law is not such an area despite a common view – based conciously or unconsciously on the idea of the 'Volksgeist' – to the contrary. It is enough to refer to the changes in Roman law in ancient Egypt, and to legitimation *per subsequens matrimonium* in Scotland because of Roman law and transported from Scotland to New Zealand and then to England. One could also refer to the acceptance in the Turkish Civil Code of 1926 of much of Swiss family law. Perhaps a little more should be said. Often family law has a particularly marked religious basis or backing, as in modern India, Ireland and Israel, and is then resistant to change of any kind, including transplants. More generally, family law tends to be conservative and hence may lag behind other parts of the law. When that happens, there may be a sudden period of change, as in the Rome of Augustus or the England of the 1920's or Turkey in 1926,[8] and family law then may be very open to transplants. Again, even such a cumbrous and far-reaching institution as feudal landownership can be transplanted, as can be seen first in its spread throughout Europe and then in its later export from England to North America and New Zealand.[9] Even if it is conceded that its spread in Europe was as one aspect of a coherent economic, social and

---

[7] *The Works of Mr. Francis Rabelais* (Urquhart's translation of 1653), second book, chapter 5.

[8] Cf. H. Timur, 'The place of Islamic law in Turkish law reform', *Annales de la Faculté de Droit de l'Université d'Istanbul*, v (1956), pp. 75ff. And for discontent and difficulties with this reception see M. R. Belgesay, 'La Réception des lois étrangères en Turquie', *Annales*, v. *cit.*, pp. 93ff at pp. 96ff; H. V. Velidedeoğlu, 'De certains problèmes provenant de la réception du Code civil suisse en Turquie', *Annales*, v. *cit.*, pp. 99ff at pp. 111ff; Z. F. Findikoğlu, 'Special Aspects of the Turkish Reception of Law', *Annales*, v. *cit.*, pp. 155ff.

[9] Of course, by the time it was exported from England it had been greatly modified.

political system rather than as simply the adoption of a body of legal rules – which is a gross oversimplification – this would not be true for its transfer to British colonies.

Seventhly, the time of reception is often a time when the provision is looked at closely, hence a time when law can be reformed or made more sophisticated. It thus gives the recipient society a fine opportunity to become a donor in its turn.

Eighthly, reception is possible and still easy when the receiving society is much less advanced materially and culturally, though changes leading to simplification, even barbarisation, will be great. A competent scholar would be able to find examples not only in fifth century Germany and mediaeval Scotland, but also in the Wild West.

Ninthly, foreign law can be influential even when it is totally misunderstood, for instance Bell and constructive delivery. It is reasonable, even if unfair, to refer here to Montesquieu and the doctrine of separation of powers. It is much disputed[10] whether Montesquieu actually misunderstood the English constitution or was constructing an ideal constitution with England as its source. However this may be, his views were of fundamental importance to the framers of the American constitution though they were under no illusion as to the true nature of the English constitution. As Madison puts it, 'The British Constitution was to Montesquieu what Homer has been to the didactic writers on epic poetry.'[11]

Tenthly, the previous two conclusions, in fact almost all so far, show the importance of authority for transplants and for law in general. It is a very marked characteristic of lawyers that they do not like to think they are standing alone or that their decisions are the result of their own limited reasoning power. Hence the strength of the doctrine of precedent in English law, the Roman jurists' habit of listing their fellows in support, and to some extent the frequency of transplants. Even when a jurist has decided what he wants the law to be, he may look for (or even invent) a precedent in a respected system to bolster his opinion. In extreme cases the claim may even be made that the law comes from a god. Transplants in fact offer an insight into the overwhelming importance of the part played by authority in law.

Eleventhly, a nation which is inventive in law may be largely free

---

[10] Cf., e.g., M. J. C. Vile, *Constitutionalism and the Separation of Powers* (Oxford, 1967), pp. 83 ff.
[11] *The Federalist Papers*, no. 47.

from accepting transplants even at a time when foreign influence is very important in other matters in the society. But this is not always the case. Late republican Rome is an instance of the first phenomenon, mediaeval England of the second.

Twelfthly, law like technology is very much the fruit of human experience. Just as very few people have thought of the wheel yet once invented its advantages can be seen and the wheel used by many, so important legal rules are invented by a few people or nations, and once invented their value can readily be appreciated, and the rules themselves adopted for the needs of many nations.

Thirteenthly, peoples develop along their own lines and to show marked cultural progress and inventiveness in one field is no indication that similar progress will be made in others. Thus, the Romans and the English, more than other European peoples, have been vitally important for the development of the traditional fields of private law. In private law, the supreme contribution of the Italian, French, Dutch, German and other European jurists has lain rather in their rationalisation, sophistication and adaptation of the rules of Roman law.[12]

To conclude the chapter on a different note. What has been said, on the one hand about the extent and ease of transplants, the deep historical roots of contemporary law and the fact that the creation of law for that precise society in which it is operating is neither always common nor very important, and on the other hand about modifications made to transplanted law, can raise questions about the possibility and desirability of a unified system of law, at least for the whole of the Western world.[13] Obviously a complete legal union is neither possible nor desirable.[14] But it would be a relatively easy task to frame

[12] But one must not forget the importance of non-Roman customs, and also the development beyond Roman law.

[13] For voluntary acceptance of Western law in non-Western countries see, e.g., F. P. Walton, 'The Historical School of Jurisprudence and Transplantations of Law', *Journal of Comparative Legislation*, ix (3rd ser.) (1927), pp. 183ff; and of Swiss and German law in Turkey see the papers presented to the Istanbul colloquium on the problem of the reception of foreign laws (September 1955) collected in *Annales de la Faculté de Droit d'Istambul*, v (1956).

[14] But unification of commercial law may be both possible and desirable. One should mention here Article 100 of the Treaty of Rome on the approximation of such legislative and administrative provisions of the Member States of the E.E.C., as have a direct incidence on the establishing or functioning of the Common Market: see now the papers collected in *Angleichung des Rechts der Wirtschaft in Europa* (Kölner Schriften zum Europarecht, no. 11, Cologne, 1971). Attention should also be directed to the numerous studies by R. David which have culmin-

a single basic code of private law to operate throughout, with each
nation being left free to modify for itself any part it found not to its
liking. Frequent revision of the basic code in the light of national
modifications would in a short period result in a virtually unitary
legal system. One might wonder, though, whether it would be worth
the effort. But equally one must wonder whether it is sensible and
worth the effort to have separate private law in each of the fifty states
of the United States of America; and to have one legal system for
Scotland and another for England and Wales, especially when there is
only one legislature. The important point here, I suggest, is not the
precise aptitude of the law for the particular territory concerned. It is
much more the psychological value of having one's own legal system.

---

ated in his *The International Unification of Private Law* which appears as chapter 5
of volume 2 of *The International Encylopaedia of Comparative Law* (Tübingen, etc.,
1971).

CHAPTER 17

COMPARATIVE LAW AND LEGAL HISTORY

This book has been concerned to show the kind of thing which may be learned about legal development from a knowledge of particular instances of a relationship between systems. The previous chapter attempted to set out some very general conclusions which might be drawn, but these must not be exaggerated. No attempt has been made to formulate a precise sociology of transplants: such an approach might be as doomed to failure as the theories of a particular pattern of development inherent in early systems of law.[1]

Earlier in the book it was stressed that the comparatist was faced with a multiplicity of choices.[2] As a result of the choices which have been made (and which derive from the author's interests) the book wears a historical guise. But such a strong emphasis is not necessary. Comparative Law as here understood is very different from Legal History, and all the relationships examined might have concerned law still very much in force. For instance, many recent Civil Codes have a close relationship to one foreign system, as that of Greece[3] to the German, that of Turkey to the Swiss, that of Ethiopia[4] to the French. But the nature of this relationship can vary greatly. The donor and the recipient system might share the same legal tradition and the former might have received its status as donor largely because it was codified first and provided a formulation which could be easily borrowed. The sole contribution of the donor might lie in the provisions of its Code or the recipient might also take account of juristic and legal developments in the donor state even after the codification there. In an extreme case the recipient might regard as directly relevant for the interpretation of its Code, interpretations made in the donor state even after the promulgation of the recipient's Code. The study of the variations in these relationships would well repay the comparatist.

---

[1] Cf. supra, pp. 12ff.   [2] Supra, pp. 18ff.

[3] A very convenient book is P. J. Zepos, *Greek Law* (Athens, 1949). Translations of the Greek Civil Code exist in German [D. Gogos, (translator), *Das Zivilgesetzbuch von Griechenland* (Berlin, 1951)] and French [P. Mamopoulos (translator), *Code Civil Hellénique* (Athens, 1956)].

[4] This Civil Code was published in Amharic and English in the official Ethiopian Gazette, the *Negarit Gazeta* (exceptional number, no. 2 of 1960). A French edition, *Code civil de l'Empire d'Éthiopie*, was published in Paris in 1962.

None the less, Comparative Law as here understood is unthinkable without history, even if only very modern history. But Comparative Law does not only take from Legal History: it can also give. Some of the reflections listed in the previous chapter may make a legal historian concerned with his own system more alert to certain aspects of the development. In this final chapter we will look at two instances (out of a great many) where not enough work has yet been done on the primary sources for all the important facts in the development to be apparent, where reflections proper to the comparatist may clarify the issues for the historian, and where the historian's results, in their turn, could be of great interest to the comparatist.

In 1808 what is now usually called the *Louisiana Civil Code*[5] was published under the title *A Digest of the Civil Laws now in force in the territory of Orleans with alterations and amendments adapted to its present system of government*. Louisiana, of course, had had a chequered history; French rule began in 1712, but Louisiana was ceded to Spain in 1762,[6] then in 1800 back to France, who transferred it to the United States in 1803. Very recently R. Batiza[7] has investigated the sources of the Code of 1808 and claims to have identified the sources of 2,081 of the 2,160 provisions; The French *Projet de Code Civil, présenté par la Commission nommée par le Gouvernement le 24 Thermidor an VIII* (1800) is the source of 807 provisions, the French *Code civil* (issued in 1804) of 709,[8] Domat of 175, Pothier of 113, Domat or Pothier of 184, the *Coutume de Paris* of 9, the *Ordonnance civile pour la réformation de la justice* (of 1667) of 6. Thus 85% of the provisions, it is claimed, have an origin in France. The remaining provisions derive, it is said, mainly from Spanish law, but also from Blackstone, from Roman law directly, from French and Spanish provisions for colonies and from Louisiana Acts. Almost 50% of the provisions of the Code of 1808 are also in the Revised Code of 1870 which is still in force.

Batiza's conclusions have been vigorously attacked by Pascal who thinks that the main origins of the substance of the Code of 1808 lie in Spanish law.[9] Who is right and who is wrong need not concern us

---

[5] But one scholar, at least, emphatically prefers to call it the Digest of 1808; R. A. Pascal, 'Sources of the Digest of 1808: A Reply to Professor Batiza', *Tulane Law Review*, xlvi (1972), pp. 603ff at p. 604, n. 4.

[6] Possession of the Colony by the Spanish Crown began only in 1769.

[7] 'The Louisiana Civil Code of 1808: its Actual Sources and Present Relevance', *Tulane Law Review*, xlvi (1971), pp. 4ff.

[8] Though many of these may have come from the *Projet*.

[9] 'Sources of the Digest of 1808.' Batiza's reply is in 'Sources of the Civil Code

at this stage. But the existence of such massive borrowing should be of great interest to a comparatist. More fascinating still is the mixture. Much would be revealed about legal development by an investigation into the circumstances in which French law or Spanish law or Blackstone or Roman law was preferred. How far was the mixture particularly adapted to life in Louisiana? To what extent does the Code of 1808 reflect the law in operation in Louisiana before its promulgation? Did the existence of convenient models in the *Projet* and the *Code civil* diminish the importance in the mixture of Spanish law? The Code of 1808 was issued in both French and English and was compiled by Louis Moreau Lislet and James Brown. Did linguistic factors influence the choice of source material?[10] Further what is one to make of the so-called de la Vergne Volume? This is an interleaved copy of the Code of 1808 which was owned by Louis Moreau Lislet, and which opposite the great majority of Articles sets out textual references to other systems, and was apparently written in 1814 by Moreau Lislet himself.[11] Again, Article 3 of the Code of 1808 accepts custom as creating law, and it derives almost verbatim from Article 5 of the French *Projet* of the year VIII (1800). Yet custom as a source of law is not mentioned in the *Code civil*, promulgated 24 Ventôse of the year XI, though the law of 30 Ventôse of the year XII declared that general or local customs should cease to have the force of law.[12] Why did Louisiana here follow the *Projet*?[13]

---

of 1808, Facts and Speculation: a Rejoinder', *Tulane Law Review*, xlvi (1972), pp. 628ff; cf. in the same issue of that journal, J. M. Sweeney, 'Tournament of Scholars over the Sources of the Civil Code of 1808', pp. 585ff.

[10] But Moreau Lislet was well acquainted with Spanish and, in collaboration with H. Carleton, translated part of *Las Siete Partidas: A Translation of the titles on promises and obligations, sale and purchase, and exchange; from the Spanish of Las siete partidas* (New Orleans, 1818).

[11] The avant-propos begins: '*Le but de cet ouvrage est de faire connaître par des nottes écrites sur des pages en blanc attachées du Digeste des Loix de cet État, quels sont les textes des loix civiles et Espagnoles, qui y ont quelque rapport.*

A cet effet, on trouvera à côté du texte anglais, une liste générale de tous les titres des loix Romaines et Espagnoles, qui sont relatifs aux matières traitées dans chaque chapitre du Digeste, et à côté du texte français et article par article, la citation des principales loix des divers codes, d'où sont tirées les dispositions de notre Statut local.' The de la Vergne volume has now been published: *A Digest of the Civil Laws now in force in the Territory of Orleans (1808)* (Baton Rouge, 1971).

[12] This law (which has become Article 7 of the present *Code civil*) was promulgated before the *Code civil* came into effect.

[13] And why has the de la Vergne volume no references to the Code civil?

The second instance is taken from Scottish criminal law. The leading exponent in the early 19th century, D. Hume, rightly denied that Roman law was authoritative in Scotland,[14] and went on to claim: 'Independently of this, the truth seems to be, that there are in every case very great obstacles to the transferring of the Criminal Law of any one nation to another. Because in any country, the frame and character of this part of its laws, has always a much closer dependence on the peculiar circumstances of the people, than the details of its customs and regulations in most of the affairs of civil life.'[15] He then stresses the differences between the Romans and the Scots, and states that if he has paid little regard to the compilations of Justinian 'still less have I thought it material to detain the reader on every occasion with a scrutiny into the sentiments of the numerous commentators on them in modern times'[16] and he explains that these authors knew nothing about the practice of Scotland. He continues: 'As Sir George Mackenzie has observed with respect to the quotation of authorities,[17] "he darkens his own cause, when just, who uses these to ignorant people; and he lessens his own esteem, who thinks he needs them among men of better sense." '

But there is something very strange here. Mackenzie's famous *Laws and Customs of Scotland in Matters Criminal*, which was published in 1678, was the first comprehensive book on Scottish criminal law, and no comparable work was published on the subject until Hume's *Commentaries*. The importance of Mackenzie's work appears only too clearly in the first pages of Hume's introduction. But contrary to what might be supposed after reading Hume's quotation from Mackenzie, the latter's treatise has very many citations of Roman law and the commentators thereon, from the Glossators and Bartolus to Gothofredus and Matthaeus. Indeed, the treatise is even subtitled 'Wherein is to be seen how the Civil Law,[18] and the Laws and Customs of other Nations do agree with, and supply ours.' Thus foreign legal rules are expressly declared to have influenced the growth of Scottish criminal law. And in the Author's Design, Mackenzie states boldly 'The Reason why I have so often cited the *Basilicks, Theophil* and the *Greek*

---

[14] *Commentaries on the Law of Scotland respecting Crimes*, 4th edit. (Edinburgh, 1844), p. 15.

[15] Ibid p. 16.

[16] Ibid p. 17.

[17] *The Works of Sir George Mackenzie*, ii (Edinburgh, 1722), p. 353.

[18] i.e. Roman Law.

Scholiasts, was not only because none before me have used them in criminal Treatises, but because I conclude then the best interpreters of *Justinian's* Text.' Records of decided cases from around that time also indicate the importance of continental authority.[19] The quotation cited by Hume does not indeed come from Mackenzie's criminal law treatise but from his *Vindication of the Government in Scotland during the Reign of King Charles II*, and, in fact, from a part in which he is justifying his own zealousness as King's Advocate in treason trials: 'In the next place I must observe, that no Nation has ever blamed a King's Advocate for assisting in criminal Processes; nor lies there any Action or Scandal against him anywhere on that account, as can be proved from many Hundreds of Citations of the best Laws and Lawiers: But he darkens his own Cause, when just, who uses these to ignorant People; and he lessens his own Esteem who thinks he needs them amongst Men of better sense. The Law trusts him entirely as a publick Servant, who manages these Pursuits by virtue of his Office, and not by Malice.' Mackenzie's stated reluctance to quote authority is to be understood within very narrow limits.

But what is the legal historian to make of this? Is he to agree with Hume that the transplanting of criminal law is extremely difficult and that it is inappropriate for a writer to refer to foreign authorities? Should he be led to believe that Scottish criminal law is very much a native product, and that the foreign authorities cited in the 17th century are referred to for decoration and support but were not influential in the development of the law? Is he to think that there was very considerable borrowing from Roman law, despite the difference in manners and life between the Romans and the Scots? Or should he think that the law borrowed by the Scots from the commentators was already very different from that which existed at Rome? Is he to look for a difference in outlook between the time of Mackenzie and the time of Hume? Why has the citation of European authority disappeared from Scottish criminal cases? In framing the questions and in evaluating the possible answers, a knowledge of Comparative Law will help the historian.

[19] See, for instance, the cases in *Selected Justiciary Cases 1624–1650*, i (Stair Society, vol. no. 16, Edinburgh, 1953); and in *Justiciary Records of Argyll and the Isles 1644–1742*, ii, *1705–1742* (Stair Society, vol. 25, Edinburgh, 1969).